The Anglo-American Winter War with Russia, 1918–1919

The Anglo-American Winter War with Russia, 1918–1919

A Diplomatic and Military Tragicomedy

Benjamin D. Rhodes

Contributions in Military Studies, Number 71

Greenwood Press
New York • Westport, Connecticut • London

Library of Congress Cataloging-in-Publication Data

Rhodes, Benjamin D.
  The Anglo-American winter war with Russia, 1918-1919.

  (Contributions in military studies, ISSN 0883-6884 ;
no. 71)
  Bibliography: p.
  Includes index.
  1. Soviet Union—History—Allied intervention,
1918-1920.   2. United States—Military relations—
Soviet Union.   3. Soviet Union—Military relations—
United States.   4. United States—History, Military—
20th century.   I. Title.   II. Series.
DK265.42.U5R46   1988   947.084'1   87-23645
ISBN 0-313-26132-6 (lib. bdg. : alk. paper)

British Library Cataloguing in Publication Data is available.

Library of Congress Catalog Card Number: 87-23645
ISBN: 0-313-26132-6
ISSN: 0883-6884

First published in 1988

Greenwood Press, Inc.
88 Post Road West, Westport, Connecticut 06881

Printed in the United States of America

The paper used in this book complies with the
Permanent Paper Standard issued by the National
Information Standards Organization (Z39.48-1984).

10 9 8 7 6 5 4 3 2 1

Copyright Acknowledgments

The author and publisher are grateful for permission to reprint portions of the following
articles by Benjamin D. Rhodes:

"A Prophet in the Russian Wilderness: The Mission of Consul Felix Cole at Archangel,
1917-1919," *The Review of Politics*, July 1984.
  "Wisconsin's War Against Russia, 1918-19," *Transactions*, 1984.
  "The Anglo-American Railroad War at Archangel, 1918-1919," *Railroad History*,
autumn of 1984.
  "The Anglo-American Intervention at Archangel, 1918-1919: The Role of the 339th
Infantry," *The International History Review*, vol. viii, no. 3, August 1986.
  "Aviation and the Anglo-American Intervention at Archangel, 1918-1919," reprinted
from AEROSPACE, Fall 1986, with permission. Copyright 1986 by the Air Force Historical Foundation. No additional copies may be made without the express permission of the
author and of the editor of AEROSPACE HISTORIAN.
  Every reasonable effort has been made to trace the owners of copyright materials in this
book, but in some instances this has proven impossible. The publishers will be glad to
receive information leading to more complete acknowledgments in subsequent printings of
the book, and in the meantime extend their apologies for any omissions.

Contents

Illustrations

Following page xii

MAPS

PHOTOS

Preface

Ill-conceived military campaigns have been anything but unique in history. But the weak Anglo-American intervention at Archangel in 1918-1919 was unusually inept based as it was upon misinformation, profound geographical and political misconceptions, and a generous supply of wishful thinking. Surely the Allies would have saved themselves much embarrassment had they followed the advice of American consul Felix Cole who warned that the invaders would be swallowed by the sheer vastness of North Russia. The prevalent mood of the region was for peace, Cole pointed out, and he accurately predicted that few Russians would volunteer to do the fighting. And General Tasker H. Bliss was certainly right when he speculated that the British (the chief sponsors of the affair) had bitten off more than they could chew. Other than accentuating Soviet paranoia about the sinister designs of the western imperialists, the Allied invasion proved a futile adventure and its obvious military lessons were promptly forgotten by both sides.

Sir Herbert Butterfield has pointed out that once the passions of battle have subsided, historiography usually evolves from heroic, black and white interpretations to an appreciation of more complex and tragic elements. In many ways the Anglo-American winter war at Archangel serves as a case in point. In the immediate aftermath many western participants looked upon their enemy as atrocity-prone desperadoes (the "Bolos") who were dominated by Germany (at least until the armistice of 11 November 1918). Today it is difficult to detect real villains on either side. Neither Commissar M. S. Kedrov nor General Aleksandr Samoilo appear more fanatical or violent than their western counterparts. Even General F. C. Poole, for all his conceit and posturing, appears more pathetic than sinister, a man who got himself into an untenable situation, who was bedeviled by blundering Russian politicians and Allied diplomats, and who was not even informed by his own government that President Wilson had restricted the American participants to the role of noncombatants. Most lonely of all was Colonel George E. Stewart, the American commander, who was sent to Archangel without adequate instructions and then kept in the dark by his government throughout the long Russian winter.

In one way or another all the participants in the affair justified their actions as logical and moral. The British War Cabinet looked upon the intervention as a plausible gamble to restore the eastern front against Germany. Viewed from London it seemed preposterous to think that the Bolsheviks could offer serious resistance to western troops and artillery. President Wilson, under pressure from the Allies, agreed only reluctantly to participate, while protesting that he still opposed intervention in principle. He defended his decision on humanitarian grounds and upon the belief that he had restricted the American participants to the role of noncombatants. Yet, as had been the case with Wilson's interventions in Mexico, moral diplomacy produced a less than moral result. In the end, America's participation did not prevent the establishment of a military dictatorship instead of democracy in North Russia, nor could it avert the eventual collapse of the White Russians. In Wilson's defense, he was immediately and thoroughly disillusioned with British policy in North Russia and sought an exit at the first opportunity.

Compared with the professional conduct of the war on the western front, the military operations in North Russia were often amateurish and sometimes absurd. Both sides were forced to rely upon untrained, poorly motivated second class troops who were outfitted with improvised equipment. Not even the talented General Edmund Ironside could accomplish military miracles under such circumstances. Still, considering the polyglot nature of the expedition and the odds against its success, the biggest surprise is not that there were a few mutinies or cases of cowardice and incompetence, but that there were not more. The conscripted American, British, White Russian, and Bolshevik forces, each mutually detesting the other, could justifiably regard themselves as players in a drama controlled by distant abstract forces beyond their control. The long suffering people of Archangel province could take a similar view. Bruce Lockhart, the British representative in Moscow, aptly described the campaign as an "unbelievable folly" that was comparable with the worst mistakes of the Crimean War. Whether the lessons of the North Russian affair were absorbed any more thoroughly than those of the Crimean conflict is questionable.

My interest in the Allied intervention in Russia originated over twenty years ago when Daniel M. Smith of the University of Colorado introduced me to George F. Kennan's monumental two-volume account of Soviet-American relations during World War I. A brilliant diplomatic study, Kennan's work made no pretense of discussing the military aspects of the intervention in any detail. Most of the historical literature on the subject, with the exception of older works by Leonid I. Strakhovsky and E. M. Halliday, has also concentrated upon the diplomatic maneuvering which preceded the Allied decision to intervene, or has emphasized the Siberian phase of the intervention, probably because more Allied troops were involved there than was the case in North Russia. That there remained a general unfamiliarity with the Anglo-American winter war against the Bolsheviks at Archangel was illustrated by a statement contained in the 1984 State of the Union Address: "It is true that our governments have had serious differences. But our sons and daughters have never fought each other in war."

I would like to express my thanks to the staffs of the Public Record Office, the National Archives, the United States Army Military History Institute, the United States Military Academy Library, and the Bentley Historical Library for their valuable assistance in my research. In particular, I am indebted to the State Historical Society of Wisconsin and the Memorial Library of the University of Wisconsin for access to their exceptional resources, without which this study could not possibly have been written. Bruce P. Flood first pointed out to me that the American troops involved in the Archangel campaign were primarily from Michigan and Wisconsin, a fact which had escaped my notice. My wife Florence suggested numerous improvements in style, form, and logic and assisted in the tedious routine of proofreading. I would like to acknowledge the support of the University of Wisconsin-Whitewater for encouraging my research through three state research grants and by assisting in the typing of the manuscript in the department of History by Marcy Glaser and Regina Brown. Finally, I would like to thank the following journals for permission to include in this manuscript material which they previously published: the Review of Politics for

"A Prophet in the Russian Wilderness: The Mission
of Consul Felix Cole at Archangel, 1917-1919," July,
1984; <u>Transactions</u> of the Wisconsin Academy of
Sciences, Arts and Letters for "Wisconsin's War
Against Russia, 1918-1919," 1984; <u>Railroad History</u>
for "The Anglo-American Railroad War at Archangel,
1918-1919," Winter, 1984; the <u>International History
Review</u> for "The Anglo-American Intervention at
Archangel, 1918-1919:   The Role of the 339th
Infantry," August, 1986; and the <u>Aerospace Historian</u>
for "Aviation and the Anglo-American Intervention at
Archangel, 1918-1919," September, 1986.   Throughout
this manuscript I have used the simplified, highly
anglicized spelling of Russian place names found
in the British and American documents.

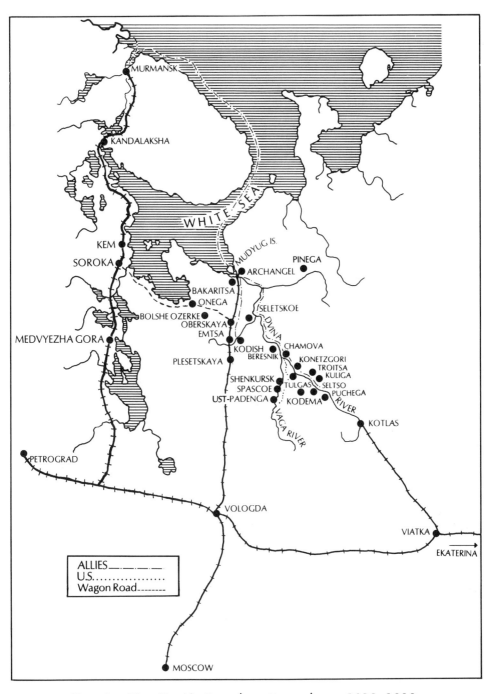

Map 1. The North Russian Campaign, 1918-1919.

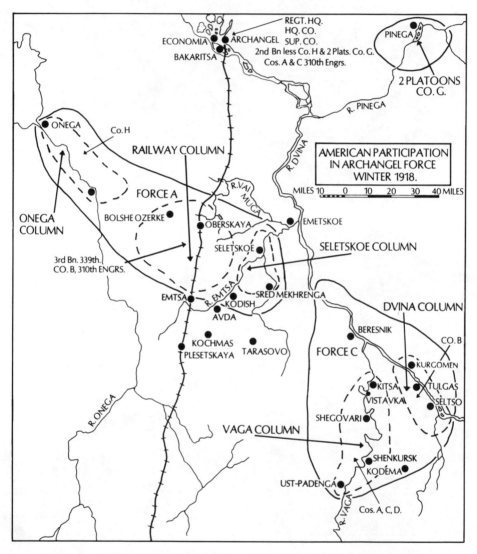

Map 2. American participation in Archangel Force.
Winter 1918.

1. General F. C. Poole and Russian officers. October, 1918. Courtesy of the National Archives.

2. The Allied diplomats and President N. V. Chaikovsky at the residence of American ambassador David R. Francis at Archangel. October 13, 1918. Bottom row, left to right, Serbian Minister Spolaikovich; member of the Archangel Provisional Government, Mr. Garodetsky; Italian Minister Torretta; President N. V. Chaikovsky; Ambassador David R. Francis; Provisional Government Minister of Finance Kourokine; British Commissioner Francis Lindley; Provisional Government Minister Mefodieff. Top row, left to right, Provisional Government Secretary Zuboff; Chinese Secretary Tchen Ten Tchai; Brazilian Chargé G. Vionna Kelsch; Provisional Government Minister Grudisteff; Earl Johnson, secretary of David R. Francis; Provisional Government Minister de Boccard. Courtesy of National Archives.

3. Reviewing the troops. Right to left: General E. Ironside; Colonel G. E. Stewart; Captain Joel R. Moore; Chargé d'Affaires DeWitt C. Poole, Jr.; Captain M. A. Goff; Major J. Brooks Nichols. November 20, 1918. Courtesy of the National Archives.

4. Reviewing the troops. Right to left: General E. Ironside; Colonel G. E. Stewart; Major F. F. Ely; Major J. Brooks Nichols; Chargé d'Affaires DeWitt C. Poole, Jr.; Captain Joel R. Moore; Captain M. A. Goff. November 20, 1918. Courtesy of the National Archives.

5. Point of farthest advance by American forces in North Russia, 28 versts from Shenkursk. The village of Pagosta in the distance was occupied by the Bolsheviks and the church towers were used as observation posts. Eleven days after this photo was taken, the Bolsheviks launched a surprise offensive that forced the Allies to abandon this point and Shenkursk as well. Photo by Sergeant Grier M. Shotwell, Signal Corps, January 8, 1919. Courtesy of the National Archives.

6. Colonel George E. Stewart. October, 1918. Courtesy of the National Archives.

7. George Evans Stewart. Summer of 1927-1928 when
commanding the 28th Infantry. Courtesy of the
U.S. Military Academy Library, West Point, New
York.

8. Felix Cole, consul general of the U.S. Lega-
tion at Warsaw, Poland. December 5, 1928.
Courtesy of the Collections of the Library of
Congress.

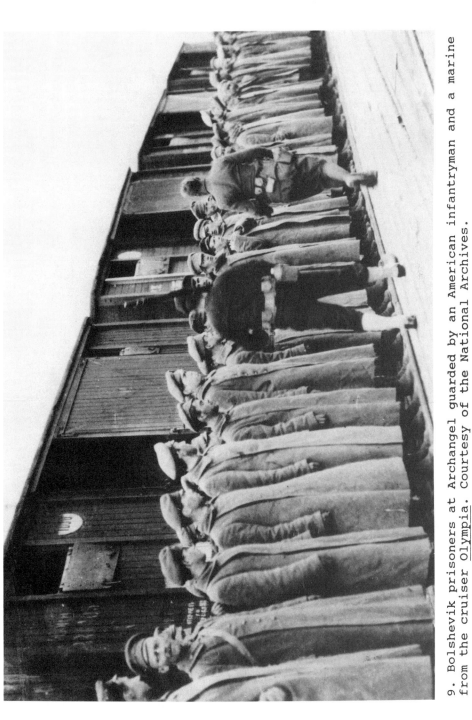

9. Bolshevik prisoners at Archangel guarded by an American infantryman and a marine from the cruiser Olympia. Courtesy of the National Archives.

10. Verst 455 Railroad Front. February 17, 1919. "I" Company is lined up preparatory to the awarding of the French Croix de Guerre to eight soldiers for bravery. Captain Horatio G. Winslow of Madison, Wisconsin is in front of the company. Six weeks later "I" Company was inaccurately accused of having mutinied. Courtesy of the National Archives.

11. Funeral procession of Lieutenant Marcus T. Casey of New Richmond, Wisconsin at Archangel, Russia. September 18, 1918. Courtesy of the National Archives.

12. American soldiers on patrol, Vologda Railroad Front. February 21, 1919. Left to right, Bugler Charles Metcalf, Private Harold Holliday, and Sergeant Ernest Reed. Courtesy of the National Archives.

13. Allied officers on the Vologda Railroad Front. February 17, 1919. Left to right, Colonel Dunlap (French), Colonel Lucas (French), General Ironside (British), Colonel George E. Stewart (American), Major C. Archer (French), Major J. Brooks Nichols (American), and Lieutenant De Reims (French). Courtesy of the National Archives.

14. Allied officers and locomotive, Vologda Railroad Front. February 20, 1919. Left to right, Lieutenant De Reims (French), Lieutenant C. J. Gardiner (American), Major J. Brooks Nichols (American), Lieutenant M. J. Carpenter (American), Lieutenant Neil C. Hallock (American). Courtesy of the National Archives.

The Anglo-American
Winter War with Russia,
1918–1919

1

The Decision to Guard
Military Stores

As they left America by troopship in the summer
of 1918, the soldiers of the United States 339th
Infantry were under the impression that they were on
their way to France to wage war against the forces of
Kaiser Wilhelm II. At the last minute, however, both
their destination and the enemy were changed. Their
exact location was now a classified secret. But, in
letters to their relatives, the soldiers described
many attractive aspects of the place. Geographically,
the country resembled the northern counties of
Michigan and Wisconsin. Forests of pine, spruce,
and aspen dominated the largely flat landscape,
which also featured numerous meadows filled with
wild flowers and unusual mosses, as well as clear
lakes and rivers. Ample wildlife made the area a
virtual paradise for the sportsman and naturalist;
the woods teemed with abundant deer, ducks, geese,
woodhens, crows, immense rabbits, and flocks of
white chickadees so plentiful that "when they flew
it looked like a snowstorm." In summer there were
long hours of daylight and mild temperatures. During
the months of intense cold the troops were housed in
snug, well-heated dwellings that were frequently
equipped with saunas. Even the long winter nights
were made memorable by brilliant displays of northern
lights. And the natives of the region were not too
much different from the people at home--hardworking,
religious folk who loved a good joke and often drank
too much.[1]
     At the same time there were drawbacks: bottomless
swamps and clouds of mosquitoes in the summer. During
the winter months homesickness and melancholia were
induced by the short days and temperatures as low
as -53° Fahrenheit. The food ration, consisting
primarily of black tea, hardtack, and canned willy
(corned beef), also left much to be desired. Flies,

fleas, cockroaches, bedbugs, and ticks were other disagreeable features. "It's the filthiest place I've ever been in," wrote one Milwaukean. "The cooties keep us dancing every minute."[2] Probably the most unattractive aspect of the mission was the imminent danger of death from sickness, mines, booby traps, and rifle and artillery fire. Tragically, for the 222 American soldiers who lost their lives, they were not engaged in practice maneuvers in the north woods, but were fighting a shooting war against the Bolsheviks more than 200 miles deep in the interior of North Russia.

America's connection with the affair originated in the distressing news that came out of Russia in the autumn of 1917. First, in November the Bolsheviks easily toppled the pro-Western Provisional Government. And within a few months, to the consternation of the Allies, the Bolsheviks betrayed the West by signing a separate peace with Germany at Brest-Litovsk (3 March 1918) and leaving the war. From the Allied viewpoint, especially that of the British War Cabinet, the Bolshevik action was intolerable, because it would permit the Germans to transfer their army to the western front and to gain control over the extensive Allied military supplies sent to Russia. The British proposed, therefore, to invade Russia through its northern ports of Murmansk and Archangel, take possession of the extensive military supplies there, and eventually reorganize the eastern front with the assistance of Russian volunteers. British planners also advocated Allied intervention in Siberia to protect military stores piled up at Vladivostok and to deny Germany the resources of the region by occupying the Trans-Siberian Railroad. With their manpower and resources thoroughly committed on the western front, the British were counting on the United States to provide the bulk of the soldiers and supplies for both the Siberian and North Russian projects.[3]

For many months the idea of military intervention in Russia met with general disapproval from Washington. Both Secretary of War Newton D. Baker and General Peyton C. March, the army's chief of staff, opposed the project as militarily unsound. Baker, who characterized the North Russian intervention as "nonsense from the beginning," recalled: "The only real disagreement I ever had with President Wilson was about the sending of American troops to North Russia." Likewise, General March argued that the war would be won or lost on the western front and on that ground he opposed "at all times the slightest diversion of our troops from that

objective." It was March's considered opinion that
military intervention in either Siberia or North
Russia would be "absolutely futile." Also
unsympathetic was General Tasker H. Bliss, the
American representative on the Supreme War Council
at Versailles. When the British in early April
attempted to ram through a policy statement approving
military intervention, Bliss refused to sign, thus
thwarting the British strategy. Finally, President
Wilson, perhaps recalling the unpleasant repercussions
that had accompanied his two military interventions in
Mexico, stubbornly resisted. Supported by Secretary
of State Robert Lansing, the president adopted a
deliberate "do nothing" policy.[4]

But the British were not easily discouraged.
Through the British ambassador, Lord Reading, and Sir
William Wiseman, a liaison agent, continuing pressure
was applied to Wilson's advisers such as Lansing and
Colonel Edward M. House. In April the president,
after at first refusing, agreed to a British request
to send a warship to Murmansk, a new port hurriedly
constructed during the war on the Kola Inlet north
of the Arctic Circle. Citing a supposed German
military threat to the region, the British had
already established a military presence at Murmansk,
consisting of a battleship and two cruisers. Two
hundred British marines were quietly landed on
6 March, and the Allied force was further strengthened
by the arrival of the French heavy cruiser Amiral
Aube. Overawed by superior force, the local Soviet
was inclined to cooperate with the Allies, although
relations with the Soviet government in Moscow became
more and more strained as British military
preparations increased.[5]

In the meantime another consideration entered
the thinking of the Allies. This factor was the
existence of the 70,000-man Czechoslovak Legion, a
well-disciplined and well-equipped survivor of the
Russian Army under the Provisional Government. In
the spring of 1918, the Czechs fled eastward from
their base in the Ukraine to escape the advancing
Germans. Their immediate destination was Vladivostok,
from where they expected to be shipped to the western
front. Under the circumstances the idea naturally
occurred to British and French military experts that
the Czechs would be very useful in protecting Russia's
northern region from the supposed German threat. On
2 May the Supreme War Council passed a somewhat vague
resolution which--without the knowledge or approval
of the Czechs--proposed splitting the Czechoslovak
Legion, with perhaps 20,000 of the troops being
transported to the northern ports. In fact, this

project existed only in the minds of its planners
and after 26 May the Czechs were engaged in open
hostilities against the Bolsheviks as they sought
to fight their way to the east.

Therefore, when the British War Cabinet on 26 May
approved the first military steps in North Russia it
acted on the basis of incomplete and misleading
information. In the first place the cabinet,
apparently mesmerized by the fury of the German
spring offensive in France, greatly exaggerated
the German threat to the northern ports. Likewise,
the British exaggerated the strength of the Czechs
and their willingness to serve the Allies. And,
consistently, the Allies seriously underestimated
the determination and ruthlessness of the Bolshevik
leadership. According to the 26 May decision of
the War Cabinet, a small expeditionary force of
approximately 1,000 troops was assigned to Murmansk
to protect the area from Germany. Also sent to
Murmansk was a 560-man training mission which was
ultimately expected to proceed in the summer to
Archangel. Presumably the Czechs, augmented by
thousands of Russian volunteers, would be organized
into an effective fighting force to thwart Germany's
designs.[6]

America's first military involvement with the
affair began with the arrival at Murmansk on 24 May
of the 5,800-ton cruiser Olympia, a vessel still
remembered for having served as Admiral George
Dewey's flagship at the battle of Manila during
the Spanish-American War. In response to British
requests to provide a warship, the Olympia had been
reassigned from convoy duty in the Atlantic and given
a hurried overhaul at the Charleston Naval Yard in
preparation for its transatlantic crossing. Under
the command of Captain Bion Boyd Bierer, the Olympia
sailed from Charleston on 28 April, arriving in
England two weeks later. After taking on coal the
ship resumed its voyage to the Arctic, arriving at
Murmansk on 24 May. On the final leg of its journey
the Olympia carried an important passenger: General
Frederick Cuthbert Poole, a forty-nine-year-old
artillery expert, who was designated "British
Military Representative in Russia." His instructions
placed him in command of all Allied forces that might
be sent to Russia and entrusted him with the training
of Russian volunteers and the Czechs, large numbers
of whom were supposed to be en route to Murmansk and
Archangel. As he contemplated his ultimate
destination, the frozen, Soviet-controlled port of
Archangel, it is at least possible that General Poole
found inspiration from a plaque attached to the deck

of the _Olympia_ marking the spot where Dewey uttered
his order, "You may fire when ready, Gridley."[7]

From the British point of view the sending of
the _Olympia_ was a welcome token of American support,
but London was counting upon a far more extensive
American commitment. As was the case throughout the
debate over Allied intervention in Russia, British
officialdom dismissed the Bolsheviks as a powerless
minority that did not need to be taken seriously.
Instead, British thinking emphasized measures that
would lead to the defeat of Germany, a nation whose
strength appeared to be expanding in the spring of
1918. By the end of May the Germans had pushed well
into the Ukraine and the Baltic provinces in the east,
while on the western front they had advanced to within
thirty-seven miles of Paris. The spring offensive
was accompanied by wild rumors that Germany intended
to seize Murmansk for use as a submarine base. To
counter this apparent threat, Arthur Balfour, the
British foreign secretary, specifically requested
that the United States send to Murmansk "a brigade,
to which a few guns should be added." The Americans
were desperately needed, said Balfour, because
Britain was "completely denuded of troops" and
because it was not practical to divert regular troops
from the western front. Without much enthusiasm
Wilson acquiesced, provided that Marshall Foch could
spare the soldiers from duty on the western front. A
further consideration was that the American soldiers
were unlikely to be exposed to much danger. As
Balfour reassuringly noted in making his request, "It
is not necessary that the troops should be completely
trained, as we anticipate that military operations in
this region will only be of irregular character."[8]

When the Supreme War Council took up the Murmansk
situation in June the British pressed their advantage
by requesting, to the great irritation of the War
Department, more American troops. Instead of one or
two battalions, Lord Milner, the war secretary, asked
for three infantry battalions, three companies of
engineers, and two artillery batteries. For the
first time the White Sea port of Archangel, still
inaccessible due to ice, entered the discussion. In
Joint Note No. 31, approved on 3 June, the Supreme
War Council recommended the occupation of Archangel
as well as Murmansk in order to check German
expansionism.[9] For the time being, Wilson resisted
British appeals to intervene in Siberia. But the
president had agreed in principle to the use of
American soldiers on Russian soil.

American diplomats in Russia added to the chorus
of interventionist advice descending upon Washington.

Since the spring of 1916 the American ambassador to
Russia had been David Rowland Francis, a sixty-four-
year-old politician and businessman from Missouri.
He was the third American ambassador to Russia within
four years and it was rumored that his predecessor
had resigned because his wife was disappointed with
the subdued social climate of wartime Petrograd. No
doubt the dismal weather of the Russian capital--
which was supposed to consist of nine months of
winter and three months of bad weather--was another
contributing factor. A native of Kentucky who
managed to work and borrow his way through Washington
University in St. Louis, Francis achieved great
financial success as a grain merchant, investor in
banking and insurance companies, and as owner of the
St. Louis Republic. His gross income, as reported on
his 1916 federal income tax return, totaled the
impressive sum of $203,823.21. While in his thirties
and forties the gregarious Francis rose quickly in
Democratic politics serving as mayor of St. Louis,
governor of Missouri, and secretary of the interior
during the last six months of Grover Cleveland's
second term. Soon his political career went into
decline as Francis was out of sympathy with the
silver wing of the Democratic party which rose to
power in the 1890s. His defeat in the Democratic
primary for the United States Senate in 1910
effectively ended his hopes for high office.[10]

His experience in business and politics and his
exuberant personality well suited Francis for the
public side of his duties. Accompanied by his black
servant Philip Jordan, Francis cut an impressive
figure as he presided over embassy social functions
or was driven in his Model T Ford to the golf course.
As befitted his age Francis played a fatherly role in
his dealings with embassy personnel, even offering
free and unsolicited advice for the resolution of
marital woes. His funeral oration delivered in
Moscow in May, 1918, following the death from a
stroke of the American consul Maddin Summers, was
both graceful and compassionate. Nor was there any
question about the ambassador's personal bravery as
he managed to survive the February and October
Revolutions of 1917, both of which were accompanied
by rioting and rifle fire in the neighborhood of the
American embassy.

By early 1918 conditions in Petrograd sharply
deteriorated. First, with a show of force, the
Bolsheviks prevented the convening of the Constituent
Assembly, a semirepresentative body elected under the
Provisional Government. And a week later Francis,
as dean of the diplomatic corps, went in person to

Lenin's headquarters where he pleaded successfully
for the release of the Rumanian minister, who had
been temporarily jailed. As the impressionable
Philip Jordan expressed it in a letter to William
Lee, one of the ambassador's St. Louis business
associates, Francis was spending much of his time
"dodging bullets." He continued,

> Mr. Lee, do you know, that this country
> is all shot to pieces. Here in Petrograd
> we are living without any law or protection
> of any kind. We are all sitting on a bomb.
> Just waiting for someone to put a match to
> it. I will put in this letter a speech that
> was made by some anarchist and that will
> give you a pretty good idea about what the
> Ambassador is up against. These people over
> here kill each other just like we swat flies
> in America. . . . When we have battles we
> do not have them out in the open but right
> in the heart of the city, just the same as
> having machine guns and cannon in front of
> the Merchants' Laclede and at Broadway and
> Washington.

Finally, on 27 February, fearing the Germans would
capture Petrograd, Francis and his staff fled by
train to the sleepy provincial capital of Vologda,
350 miles to the east.[11]

The public Francis and the private Francis appear
to have been two distinctly different persons. In
his memoirs, Francis assures the reader that he was
alert to the fact that the capital was "honeycombed
with German spies" and "as a result I was on the
lookout for the activities of such persons." He
neglected to mention, however, that in the absence
of his wife, he became infatuated with Madame Matilda
de Cramm, a Russian resident of Petrograd who was
suspected of being a German spy. Francis often
called upon her in order, he said, to take French
lessons. She was often present at the embassy and
Francis even permitted her to have access to the code
room. Despite numerous warnings from Washington,
Francis defended Madame de Cramm's innocence and
continued to write and visit her even after the
embassy had moved to Vologda. Other indiscretions
on Francis's part included flagrant speculation in
Russian currency and misuse of the diplomatic pouch
to conduct private business. Much of his time was
spent worrying about his declining business affairs
at home. When one son lost $12,000 in wheat trading,
an enraged Francis pointed out that the loss amounted

to more than two-thirds of his year's salary as
ambassador to Russia. Even more troubling were the
chronic losses (averaging between $50,000 and $60,000
a year) of the St. Louis Republic. "You know how
much I dislike to lose money," he wrote to his son
Perry, "and how much I dislike to see one of you lose
it, but grinding as that is, it does not compare in
the humiliation I undergo in seeing any enterprise
with which my name is connected become a failure."
Francis was also bothered by problems with his health.
In April, the ambassador suffered a debilitating
attack of diarrhea and soon began experiencing
serious problems with an enlarged prostate gland--a
condition which within six months brought an end to
his diplomatic career.[12]

On the all-important question of Allied military
intervention in Russia, Francis had some difficulty
in making up his mind. In February, when the Germans
had appeared ready to occupy Petrograd, Francis had
advised Washington to intervene militarily both in
North Russia and at Vladivostok. After the move to
Vologda, Francis reversed himself--apparently because
the German advance failed to materialize--and withdrew
his recommendation. For the next few weeks Francis
tried to straddle the issue, maintaining that
intervention should be resorted to only if the Allies
were invited in by the Soviets or if the Soviets
promised not to offer opposition.[13] But Francis had
a reputation for agreeing with the last person to
speak with him and soon he began listening to the
interventionists in the diplomatic community.

One source of pressure came from the French
ambassador, Joseph Noulens, who arrived at Vologda
on 29 March. A bitter foe of bolshevism and an
advocate of intervention, Noulens skillfully applied
intellectual and psychological leverage on Francis.
At the same time Francis received a barrage of
interventionist advice from the American consuls,
DeWitt Poole, Maddin Summers, Ernest L. Harris,
and the counselor of embassy, J. Butler Wright.
By 13 April Francis was once again leaning toward
intervention and advised Washington: "I think time
is fast approaching for Allied intervention and Allies
should be prepared to act promptly." And on 2 May
Francis completely capitulated and wired Secretary
of State Lansing: "In my judgement, time for Allied
intervention has arrived."[14] Left unstated by the
ambassador, as he wrote from Vologda, was precisely
where the intervention should occur.

Under normal circumstances the Allies might have
considered sending a military expedition to Moscow
via Russia's Baltic or Black Sea ports. But since

both areas were closed by World War I only one
logical point of attack remained: the White Sea
port of Archangel which was linked by rail to Moscow
700 miles to the south. Archangel was an ancient
sprawling city of about 50,000 which extended for
6 miles along the Dvina River near its outlet to
the White Sea. For many years prior to World War I
the city had been in a state of decline as much of
Russia's commerce had shifted to the more convenient
warm water ports of the Baltic. Moreover, Archangel's
usefulness as a port was hampered by its close
proximity to the Arctic Circle. Even in the best
years navigation was possible for only six or seven
months before ice terminated the shipping season.

World War I restored Archangel to a position
of prominence. In 1915 more than half of Russia's
exports (lumber, flax, grain cakes, seal skins, flour,
and naval stores) passed through Archangel. At the
same time, Allied shipping brought to the port huge
supplies of munitions, food, and fuel. Enormous
disorganization was inevitable, since the single-track
railroad was equipped to send only one passenger
train and seventy carloads of freight to the south
each day. The obvious remedy for Archangel's
overcrowding was to increase the carrying capacity
of the railroad by converting from narrow gauge to
the Russian broad gauge of five feet. This project,
which included the construction of sidings at
five-mile intervals, was finally completed in January
1916. However, due to the inadequate roadbed and
antique wood-burning locomotives, speeds were limited
to thirty miles per hour. One astonished American
observer, noting the "obsolete rolling stock, rickety,
tumbled down cars and wood-burning locomotives of a
type used in this country [the United States] fifty
years ago," thought he had stumbled upon a museum.
And, according to the American railroad expert John
F. Stevens, the railroads of Russia consisted of
"strings of match boxes coupled with hairpins and
drawn by samovars." Thus, by November 1917 the
confusion at Archangel was worse than ever as more
than 162,000 tons of munitions and metals clogged the
port and its vicinity.[15]

At first the Bolshevik Revolution was a bit slow
to penetrate to the North. For several days following
the overthrow of the Provisional Government, Archangel
was cut off from communication with either Petrograd
or Moscow, and anti-Bolshevik elements used the
interim to organize the Revolutionary Committee.
Formed out of elements that were in power under
the Provisional Government, the objective of the
Revolutionary Committee was to maintain the status

quo. In this it succeeded at first as for three
months not a single decree of the Bolsheviks was in
force in Archangel. And, for the most part, reported
consul Felix Cole, "perfect order" was maintained.
The sole exception was an unsuccessful attempt by
demobilized soldiers to pillage grain alcohol stocks
that were stored at the docks prior to export to
England.[16]

By the end of January 1918, however, the anti-
Bolshevik forces were losing their grip. The 6,000
pro-Bolshevik sailors of the White Sea fleet began,
as Cole noted, "to conduct themselves more and more
arrogantly," and demanded that the naval commander-
in-chief at Archangel turn over to them a consignment
of 6,000 revolvers held in customs. For the time
being the Bolsheviks were thwarted, as the weapons,
with which it was intended later to equip anti-
Bolshevik troops, were moved to a different warehouse.
Following the arrival of Commissar Mikhail Sergeevich
Kedrov, regarded by American ambassador Francis as
"one of the most violent and unscrupulous members
of the Bolshevik Party," the authority of the
Revolutionary Committee collapsed.[17]

On 8 February the Bolsheviks easily took control
of Archangel. First of all a telegram arrived from
Moscow abolishing the office of naval commander-in-
chief. Second, the Archangel Soviet outflanked
the Revolutionary Committee by simply voting the
committee out of existence. "And now," reported
Cole, "thanks to the moderation and good sense of a
few of the [Bolshevik] leaders, this has taken place
bloodlessly, without violence or disorder, by a mere
vote in the council [of Workmen's and Soldiers'
Deputies] and a telegram from Moscow." To the great
irritation of the Allies, the Bolsheviks began with
great determination to use the dilapidated Vologda-
Archangel Railroad to ship southward the military
stores sent to Archangel for the Provisional
Government. This confiscation, combined with the
Bolsheviks' signing of a separate peace with Germany
at Brest-Litovsk on 3 March, intensified the Allied
pressures upon Washington to intervene so as to
prevent the supplies from falling into the hands
of Germany.[18] Archangel was the logical base for
a military expedition to North Russia, and the most
obvious route southward toward Vologda and Moscow was
the railroad.

A far different view of the situation was taken
by the thirty-year-old American consul at Archangel,
Felix Cole. In his opinion economic aid to the
North, especially in foodstuffs, would do far more
to maintain Allied influence than the use of force.

Coincidentally, Cole was a native of Missouri, the
same state in which Ambassador Francis had risen to
prominence. Born in St. Louis on 12 October 1887,
he was the son of Theodore Cole, a prominent legal
bookseller and authority on statute law who later
moved his residence and business to Washington, D.C.
     For one year (1905-1906) Cole attended his
father's alma mater, the University of Wisconsin,
where he took courses in music and the liberal arts.
He finished his undergraduate education at Harvard
University, graduating <u>cum</u> <u>laude</u> in 1910 with a B.A.
degree in philosophy. <u>His first</u> job was as a reporter
and editorial writer for the <u>Boston Herald</u>. Then in
1913 the twenty-six-year-old Cole abruptly moved to
St. Petersburg, Russia, to seek his fortune. For a
few months he was employed as an automobile salesman
and then by the Argus Printing and Publishing Company,
which produced a monthly magazine in Russian under
English editorial direction. Neither position appears
to have proved a financial bonanza, but Cole did
acquire a good command of the Russian language and
also a Russian wife. Presumably it was the need for
steady employment that led Cole to become a clerk in
the American consulate at Petrograd (as the capital
was renamed in 1915). His appointment was effective
on 1 January 1917; after eight months, just before
being sent to Archangel, Cole was promoted to vice-
consul, and in March 1918, he was highly pleased when
he was advanced to consul of class 8. In a mood of
elation Cole wrote to Washington: "The attainment of
what has been my ruling ambition for the past three
years, since I first entered the Petrograd consulate
as a clerk, will not lessen my efforts for the
advancement of the Service and of the United States,
but will rather confirm me in them and stimulate."[19]
     Since the summer of 1916 the United States had
been represented at Archangel by a citizen of
Denmark, Carl Christianovitch Schulzberg-Loewe, who
preferred to sign himself simply Carl Loewe.
Together with his son Sven, Loewe operated a marine
insurance agency located on the main boulevard of
Archangel, the Troitski Prospect. Since the position
of American consular agent carried with it no salary
or housing allowance and only about $400 a year in
fees, his main source of employment was serving as a
marine-loss adjuster for three insurance companies.
After America entered the war in April 1917, Loewe,
according to the American commercial attaché at
Petrograd, showed "great interest and initiative"
in seeking to expand American trade through the
port of Archangel.[20] Soon, however, the Petrograd
embassy changed its opinion of Loewe as a mass of

circumstantial evidence accumulated that raised
serious questions about his loyalty.

The first suspicions were aroused in April
when, during the search of an apartment occupied
by a suspected spy, the name and address of "Loewe-
Archangel" was discovered. Then in June, Loewe
visited the Archangel Counter Espionage Bureau
and "insistently urged" that he be appointed as
the interpreter in all dealings between the bureau
and the American passport control officer, Hugh S.
Martin. As it turned out the bureau already had
an interpreter and Loewe was turned down. Another
suspicious development was the interception by
Russian military censors of a letter written by one
of Loewe's employees, which contained the statement:
"Loewe is considered to be a rascal and is suspected
of being a spy. No matter how regrettable, that is
nevertheless a fact." The last straw came in early
September when the American freighter Harburg docked
at Archangel and the captain told Loewe that he
had heard the signals of a German submarine while
navigating through a heavy fog. When the captain
said he would report the location to the British
naval authorities, Loewe rejoined, "Don't do that.
You will get only one thing by that, that all those
bloody English boats will go in that direction."[21]

The decision to replace Loewe with Cole was made
by the Petrograd embassy soon after a letter arrived
from Martin reporting the Harburg incident. But when
Cole set out by rail for Archangel via Vologda on
20 September, no one bothered to inform him of the
reason Loewe was being replaced. At Vologda, while
Cole waited for the cars from Moscow to be joined
to the train, the southbound train from Archangel,
on which Loewe happened to be a passenger, arrived.
Cole then produced for Loewe the letter replacing
him as consular agent. Except for a trembling of the
hands, Loewe displayed little emotion. Until Loewe's
train departed, Cole engaged him in conversation
about the overcrowded conditions at Archangel. Cole's
object was to prevent Loewe from telegraphing his son
since Cole was afraid that Sven Loewe would be
instructed to lock him out of the consular offices.
This tactic seems to have worked as Sven Loewe was
friendly and agreed to permit Cole to stay overnight.
It was only after his arrival that Cole learned from
Hugh Martin, who had rented a room from the Loewes,
of the statements made by the captain of the Harburg.
"Had I known of this matter," reported Cole on
25 September, "I should never have gone to Loewe's
even for one night, but being there, in the absence of

hotel accommodations, I decided to remain until I got a decent room, which I have been able to do today."

Before going to Archangel, Cole intended simply to take over Loewe's position and operate the consular agency from the existing office. But, because of Loewe's questionable loyalty and general unpopularity, Cole concluded that it was absolutely essential that "an entirely separate office, physically as well as 'politically' be maintained."[22] Cole now determined to ignore Loewe as much as possible. Nevertheless, Loewe's questionable activities, as observed by the Counter Intelligence Bureau, kept Cole from completely losing sight of the former consular agent. First, Loewe tried unsuccessfully to become the American Red Cross representative at Archangel. Then on 1 October Loewe tried to secure from the chief of marine transport maps showing the location of frequently used shipping channels in the White Sea. When inquiries were made, Cole pointed out that the consular agency had no need whatsoever for such maps.[23] Although Loewe's disloyalty was never conclusively established, Cole obviously displayed good judgment by keeping his distance.

Prior to the Bolshevik Revolution, Cole was primarily occupied with the commercial and bureaucratic aspects of his position. In order to emphasize his separation from the discredited Loewe, Cole rented a one-story building to house the consulate, which was now upgraded from its former status of a consular agency. Three of the six rooms were used for office space, the remainder as Cole's quarters. Later when the occupant of the adjacent apartment fled, Cole was able to rent an additional six rooms. However, judging from the inventory of equipment filed by Cole, the consulate was very meagerly furnished with plain pine tables and chairs, a stationery cabinet in "bad" condition, two typewriters, and two American flags, one listed as "torn, dirty." To refurbish the place Cole requested from the State Department a new set of chairs, a locking desk and filing cabinets, a wall clock, a thick red rug to cover the cold floors, and portraits of Presidents Wilson, Washington, and Lincoln. Washington, however, turned down the requests due to "an insufficiency of funds." Nevertheless, Cole was permitted to drop from his inventory a thirty-foot- high flagstaff, which it was deemed impractical to move to the new location, as well as an obsolete sign reading "Consular Agency."[24]

During his first two months at Archangel, before the closing of the port for the winter, Cole spent most of his time dealing with ordinary consular

matters. On five separate occasions American naval
captains appeared before him to file "Marine Notes of
Protest," which certified as to the damage suffered by
the hulls, steering gear, and cargoes of their vessels
during the month-long voyage from America. He had to
deal also with representatives of the American Red
Cross and Young Men's Christian Association,
facilitate the distribution to local theaters of
propaganda films produced by George Creel's Committee
on Public Information, and correspond with American
firms seeking to export to Russia such products as
mattress stuffing, dairy equipment, beekeeping
supplies, and metal grinding and polishing machines.
After the return of Hugh Martin to Petrograd, Cole
also had to take over the issuance of visas and
passports. And on one occasion the consulate had to
supervise the burial of an American seaman who died
at Archangel of natural causes. Through no fault of
the consulate, the body of a Russian was mistakenly
buried under the name of the American. Three days
later, when the consulate learned of the error, the
American sailor, whose frozen corpse had been lying
all the time in a cemetery shed, finally received a
proper burial.[25]

With the reduction of commercial traffic through
Archangel due to the development of winter ice, the
press of Cole's consular duties was greatly reduced.
More and more his attention was drawn to political
matters, especially after the wholly unexpected
Bolshevik overthrow of the Provisional Government on
7 November 1917. As the sole American observer in
the Russian North, Cole was in a unique position to
witness the gradual spread of the revolution to the
North and the resulting confiscation of the Allied
military stores at Archangel by the Bolsheviks. As
the man on the spot he was able to appreciate better
than more distant observers how shaky was the
Bolshevik grip on the North and how dependent the
area was on the Allies for its food. Therefore, at
a time when the Allies began to advocate military
intervention, Cole suggested an alternative policy
for keeping the Russian interior pro-Allied. What
Cole advocated was the shipment of foodstuffs "which
would make the name 'America' and 'United States'
popular and universally known in the North of Russia."
In Cole's opinion, the sending of a few cargoes of
food to Archangel would be a cheap form of American
propaganda. "The tremendous advertising power of a
few shiploads of food," he concluded, "is well worth
weighing and can hardly be exaggerated."[26]

Ambassador Francis, who was having trouble making
up his own mind on the subject of intervention,

listened respectfully to Cole's views. In March the
ambassador adopted Cole's suggestion that two cargoes
of food be dispatched to Archangel. "I recommend
granting thereof," he advised Secretary of State
Robert Lansing, "because [they] will relieve hunger
and be good propaganda." A further consideration was
that if it became necessary to evacuate the embassy
from Vologda, Archangel was the logical point of
departure and the American diplomats would likely
need all the good will that could be created. But,
due to a lack of shipping, the State Department
replied that provisioning Archangel was out of the
question. A month later Cole traveled to Vologda,
accompanied by five members of the Russian American
Committee of Archangel, and the group discussed with
Francis plans for developing trade with America in
metal, ores, and flax. Presumably Cole also used
the occasion to reiterate his opposition to military
intervention. "Cole," reported the ambassador, "has
good judgment and knows Archangel conditions."[27]

Cole's supreme demonstration of good judgment
came in the form of a cogently reasoned and well
written summation of the case against military
intervention. Cole must have invested weeks of
thought in this lengthy epistle before submitting
it to Francis on 1 June 1918, nine days after the
ambassador had cabled Washington to advise a policy
of intervention. Cole's main theme was that America's
basic interests would best be served by continuing the
existing policy of nonrecognition of the Bolsheviks
while seeking to develop as much trade as possible.
He viewed Russia as being once and for all out of
the war and as "down and out economically and
financially--at Germany's mercy now and for a long
time to come." The way to make Russia independent
of Germany, he felt, was through large-scale trade
with the Bolsheviks. "We can make more friends in
Russia," he concluded, "by the proper use of sugar,
boots, fishnets, and machinery than 200,000 or
500,000 troops."

Cole also asked Francis to consider a second major
point: that military intervention was likely to "go
further than at first planned involving unforeseen and
difficult expenditures of ships, men, and materials."
By stooping to the use of force the Allies would lose
their moral superiority over Germany and begin
relations with the new Russia on the wrong foot.
If the Allies resorted to force, Cole concluded:

>   We shall have sold our birthright in
> Russia for a mess of pottage. The birthright
> is the future friendship and economic

cooperation with a great and free democracy
controlling untold riches. The pottage will
be the recovery of a few thousand tons of
materials that we once gave to Russia after
deciding we could ourselves do without them,
the temporary control (for we do not intend
annexation) of some hundreds of square miles
of forest and barren northern tundra,
trackless and as yet unproductive, a new
front to drain our none-too-great resources
for the war, and the thanks of a few
discredited politicians without constituents.

Cole would not rule out the stationing of a strong
American naval force in North Russian waters, but
"the time for soldiers in Russia has gone beyond
recall."[28]
  After two weeks of silence from Vologda, Cole
renewed his campaign to convince Ambassador Francis
that nonintervention was the wisest policy. He also
reiterated his view that the Allies should "attempt
to bribe the local population" through shipments of
food. As Cole indelicately expressed it:

The Russian is inert, passive and very
prone to suspicion as he judges others by his
own inherent dishonesty of character. But
if he be once shown the clear road to his
own physical well-being, he will follow it
gladly. The whole course of Russian history
since the beginning of the failure of the
Russian industrial and economic machine
to keep up with the pace of the war has
turned on the stomachs of the people. The
Revolution itself, the desertion from the
army, the success of the Bolshevik movement
have been exclusively "stomach" movements,
or better "empty stomach" movements. The
North's empty stomach will bring it into
the Allied camp if the offer be made.

Moreover, argued Cole on 19 June, the Allies should
provision Archangel province to prevent the area
from becoming a source of weakness should the Allies
decide to intervene. "I have always maintained,"
Cole concluded, "that it was a good political move
to humor the North with food shipments. Now it has
become a military necessity."[29]
  By now Cole was well aware that Francis had
rejected his recommendations. On 13 June, in a
hastily drafted but good-humored and conciliatory
letter, the ambassador informed Cole: "I have read

with great interest your argument against Allied
intervention and while I admit it has great merit
I cannot agree with the conclusions." But the
arguments cited in the letter must have left Cole
just as skeptical of the conclusions reached by
Francis as Francis was unconvinced by those of Cole.
First of all, said Francis, the immediate reason for
his recommendation was a report--an inaccurate one as
it turned out--that the Germans intended to demand the
evacuation of Murmansk. A second major reason cited
by Francis for intervention was expediency. In his
opinion the Soviets were on the verge of collapse.
Supposedly Lenin had remarked, "We admit we are a
corpse but no one has the courage to bury us." To
this Francis added the notation: "Sometimes a corpse
becomes so putrid that it should be removed in the
interest of public health or for sanitary reasons.
In my judgment that is the condition now." Other
unspecified reasons had also influenced his decision,
Francis vaguely concluded, "but I have not time to
mention them."

Throughout the letter the ambassador's tone, as
befitted a professional politician, was considerate
and inoffensive. Would Cole, using a phrase once
made famous by the Republican politician James G.
Blaine, please "Burn this letter"? Would it be
advisable to send a diplomatic pouch to Washington
by means of a British steamer bound for Montreal?
Finally, Francis had a favor to ask. Would Cole try
to locate some gasoline for the ambassador's 1916
Model T Ford which had been shipped from Petrograd
to Vologda? "I had no gasoline for several weeks,"
noted Francis, "and that which I finally procured in
Petrograd was mis-named gasoline." However, Cole
found that his English source of gasoline had
disappeared and not until five weeks had passed was
he able to supply the desired commodity. In return
a delighted Francis gave instructions to scour
Vologda for scarce butter and eggs which were then
sent to Cole by courier.[30]

Not so tolerant of Cole's noninterventionist
views was consul DeWitt C. Poole, Jr., who regarded
Cole's report as "an excellent illustration of the
danger of discussing general problems from a local
point of view." Cole's greatest error, said Poole,
was his failure to recognize that the Allies had
available in Siberia "a splendid army" which could
be counted upon to tie down many German soldiers.
(Poole was referring to the Czechoslovak Legion--an
anti-Bolshevik group of former war prisoners that was
fighting its way across Siberia to Vladivostok; he,
like most western observers, exaggerated its military

strength.)   At the same time Poole recruited consul
F. Willoughby Smith to join in the assault upon
"Cole's on-the-whole-too-clever exposition of the
subject."   Smith likewise found Cole's report to be
badly flawed and superciliously stated, "Though its
logic rings more or less true to a person absolutely
ignorant of the general situation, it is not worth
serious attention."   In the overly optimistic opinion
of Smith, intervention would cause large numbers of
Russian troops to rally around the Allies.   Moreover,
a successful military campaign was practically
guaranteed by the weak condition of the Soviet Army.
"Any military demonstration on their part. . . can
be discounted," Smith concluded.

Poole then presented Francis with the hostile
critiques drafted by Smith and himself and urged that
"a restraining hand" be applied in the interest of
"principle and service discipline."   Specifically,
Poole recommended that Cole "should have strict
instructions" to communicate directly to the State
Department "only purely news items of an urgent
character."   And in a scribbled postscript written
on 6 July 1918 Poole lamented, "Unfortunately Cole's
report is probably arriving in Washington about
now."[31]   In reality, Poole's fears proved unfounded
as Cole's report was mailed by Francis, rather than
cabled, and did not arrive in Washington until
19 July after President Wilson had made his decision.
The agreeable ambassador at least had the good
judgment to reject the vindictive advice of DeWitt
Poole that Cole should be silenced for having dared
to offer dissenting opinions.   Nevertheless, Francis's
inexcusable delay in transmitting Cole's memorandum
came at a critical time, since President Wilson was
still in the process of making up his mind in June
and the first part of July.

From all sides President Wilson found himself
subjected to more intensive pressure than ever to
accept intervention.   Wilson's trusted adviser Colonel
Edward M. House, the State Department, the Supreme
War Council, the British and French governments,
Ambassador Francis and his colleagues in Russia all
appealed for American participation in the proposed
Siberian and North Russian projects.   Secretary of
War Newton D. Baker and Chief of Staff General Peyton
March offered some objections on military grounds.
But only Felix Cole had taken the pains to think
through all the facets and likely perils of the
proposed intervention.   Whether the president would
have adopted the dissenting views of an obscure
thirty-year-old consul seems somewhat unlikely.
Yet, had the president been given the opportunity

to read Cole's brilliant memorandum of 1 June
1918 it conceivably could have made a difference.
Justifiably Wilson could have described Cole, using
the same words he applied to General Tasker Bliss, as
"a remarkable man. Every word he writes strengthens
my impression that he is a real thinking man, who
takes the pains to think straight."[32]

While Cole's dispatch was slowly making its way to
Washington, the president, against his better judgment
and without much conviction, abandoned his "do
nothing" policy. He first gave way on the question
of Allied intervention in Siberia. On the evening
of 6 July Wilson called to the White House Secretary
of State Lansing, Secretary of War Baker, Secretary of
the Navy Josephus Daniels, Admiral William S. Benson,
and General March. According to March's account, the
president entered the room holding a pad in his hand
and lectured the assemblage "somewhat in the manner
of a school teacher addressing a class of pupils."
Reading from an aide-mémoire, Wilson announced that
he would send American troops to Vladivostok but
would restrict their role to guarding military stores
and to assisting the Russians in organizing their
self-defense. Even Wilson seems to have regarded
the venture as a gamble. Observing March shaking
his head in opposition to the deployment of troops,
Wilson surmised that the general feared Japan would
exploit the situation to seek territorial gains.
"Well," remarked the president, "we will have to
take that chance."[33]

Two days later Wilson admitted to his close friend
Colonel Edward House that he had been "sweating blood"
over the question of intervention. The president
remarked to Josephus Daniels that the advice of the
Supreme War Council was so impractical "that he often
wondered whether he was crazy or whether they were."
As late as 12 July, Sir William Wiseman found Wilson
still hesitant and fearful that American participation
would overcommit his administration. Finally, on
17 July Wilson tried to end the months of indecision
by writing out a complicated aide-mémoire that
incorporated many of the ideas previously discussed
during the White House meeting described by General
March. Under the signature of the secretary of state,
the document was then sent to the Allied ambassadors.
Unfortunately, the logic of the president's lengthy
statement proved very difficult to follow. At the
outset Wilson clearly stated the desire of the United
States to cooperate "ungrudgingly" and "in every
practical way" with the Allies. He then rejected
the basic premise of Allied policy by announcing his
"clear and fixed judgment" that military intervention

would exploit rather than serve Russia and would
contribute nothing to the main Allied goal of
defeating Germany. He also endorsed Allied assistance
to the Czechs on humanitarian grounds. However,
stated Wilson, the United States would not "take part
in organized intervention in adequate force from
either Vladivostok, or Murmansk and Archangel."
Finally the president denied any intention to
intervene in the internal affairs of Russia and he
made a thinly veiled threat to withdraw from the
entire venture should the Allies misuse the American
troops destined for Russian soil. On this latter
point the president would have profited from reading
Felix Cole's warning that "an expedition into Russia
could not be withdrawn in a night or a week or a
month--especially after Archangel freezes and the
neck of the White Sea clogs with ice."[34]

Certainly, it was Wilson's intention to set strict
limits on the American role. But the president's own
words were decidedly contradictory and ambiguous. On
the one hand he announced that "military intervention
would add to the present sad confusion in Russia
rather than cure it." But at the same time he
approved the use of American troops for the purpose
of guarding military stores, assisting the Czechs,
and training the Russians in self-defense. Thus, by
trying to straddle the question, Wilson contributed
to the "sad confusion in Russia" that he sought to
clarify. In its planning of the Archangel campaign
the War Office seems not to have taken seriously the
fine line that Wilson tried to draw between opposing
military intervention in principle and permitting the
landing of American troops for guard duty and training
purposes. The War Office thought so little of the
aide-mémoire that it didn't even bother to forward
a copy to General F. C. Poole who within two weeks
would launch an attack upon the Bolshevik defenders
of Archangel. In view of the advanced military
preparations the British were inclined to read only
the parts of the aide-mémoire that approved the use
of American troops and to skip lightly over the rest.

2

An Invitation to Land

Neither side was well prepared on the eve of the
Archangel campaign. At Murmansk General Poole had
available for a landing party only about 1,450 men.
Two-thirds consisted of "B" grade Royal Scots who
were supposedly fit only for garrison duty. About
500 members of the French foreign legion, who arrived
on 26 July, were available as well. Poole could also
call upon 100 Royal Marines and 50 sailors from the
Olympia. This tiny force was considerably bolstered
by the presence of the 2,670-ton scout cruiser
Attentive, which was armed with ten twelve-pound
guns, the 3,070-ton seaplane carrier Nairana equipped
with seven Short aircraft, and the French heavy
cruiser Amiral Aube. In their planning of the
campaign General Poole and Admiral Thomas Kemp faced
a formidable geographical problem: Archangel could
not be attacked directly since it was isolated from
the open sea by a twenty-five-mile channel. This
passageway could be easily mined, and the banks were
lined with heavy forest cover that was ideal for
concealing defenders. Furthermore, before entering
the channel the Allied ships would have to pass the
heavily fortified Mudyug Island. All these
considerations led Poole and Kemp to plan a coup.[1]
    The uprising was organized by a dashing Russian
naval captain, Georgi Ermolaevich Chaplin, who met
with Admiral Kemp in late June aboard the latter's
yacht at Archangel. His main problem--one which was
soon to bedevil the British--was the overwhelming
apathy among the Archangel population. In one sense
though, Archangel's "cowardice" was justified as it
was only realistic of the population not to take sides
prematurely. As the plan evolved, the head of the
new government was to be a prominent socialist, the
seventy-year-old Nicholas V. Chaikovsky, who arrived
at Archangel in late July. Noted for his flowing

white beard and blue eyes, Chaikovsky had been a
prominent member of the Constituent Assembly. As
a result of twenty-six years of exile in England
and six in America, the old man possessed a fluent
command of English, a considerable asset in view
of the forthcoming Anglo-American intervention.
According to Ambassador Francis, Chaikovsky was "an
able writer, a fine character and a valuable man."
Some idea of his less than practical outlook can be
glimpsed from his four years at Independence, Kansas
(1875-1879) where he had tried and failed to found
a religious sect. That he retained much of his
missionary nature was demonstrated by his continued
belief, as quoted by Francis, "that God is in
everyman's soul, and that is the sole existence of
what the religious denominations call the Supreme
Being." Convinced that the human race was incapable
of appreciating his beliefs, he abandoned religion
for politics.[2]

Fortunately for the plans of General Poole,
the Bolsheviks at Archangel were weak and divided.
Commissar Kedrov found himself frustrated by the
determined apathy of the population--the same problem
that impeded Chaplin. The Archangel Soviet, Kedrov
discovered, was more concerned by shortages of food
and manufactured goods than by the possibility of an
Allied invasion. Outwardly the Bolsheviks adopted
a tough position. In response to a telegram from
Trotsky, Kedrov presented Felix Cole with a letter
(delivered on 23 June at nine o'clock in the evening)
demanding the immediate withdrawal of all Allied
warships from Archangel. Three days later Kedrov
declared martial law and ordered an immediate state
of battle readiness. And on 22 July, as evidence
accumulated of British military preparations along
the west coast of the White Sea, Kedrov informed
Cole that "an almost de facto state of war" was in
existence. In reality, however, the tough talk
masked an underlying state of weakness. Only with
great difficulty was Kedrov able to pressure the
Archangel Soviet into declaring martial law; the
resulting mobilization campaign failed spectacularly,
and even the fortification of Mudyug Island fell
behind schedule. The obstacle in this case was
not apathy, but fierce swarms of mosquitoes. The
installation of mosquito netting enabled the workers
to complete the improvised defenses, which consisted
of a battery of four six-inch guns on the northern
tip of the island and an identical battery placed a
mile to the south. In their amateurish attempts at
fortification the Bolsheviks failed to consider that
if the southern battery were forced to fire at a

target north of the island, the more northerly guns would then be within the field of fire.   In such a case the guns to the south could not be fired without threatening the exposed gun crews to the north.[3]

A final warning to the Bolsheviks that Allied military action was imminent was the departure from Vologda on 24 July of David R. Francis and the other Allied ambassadors.   Fearing for their lives following the murder of the Tsar and his family, the ambassadors demanded a special train to take them to Archangel. Halfway to their destination they briefly met Kedrov, who was en route to Moscow to report to Lenin.   To the great relief of the ambassadors, who were worried that they might be imprisoned as hostages, Kedrov permitted the diplomats to continue on their way to Archangel.   After a two-day debate with the Bolshevik authorities at Archangel, who imposed various bureaucratic obstacles but did not physically detain the party of 140, the diplomats were allowed to depart for Kandalaksha on the White Sea.   Arriving at their destination Ambassador Francis and the British representative Francis Lindley advised General Poole by telephone to take immediate action, since the coup at Archangel was about to be discovered and suppressed by the Bolsheviks.[4]

Upon hearing from Lindley, Poole boldly decided to attack at once instead of waiting until 3 August as originally planned.   Reflecting two months later about his decision, Poole wrote: "It was, naturally, a considerable risk; but as I could expect no more reinforcements before the end of August, and as the opposition to us was daily growing stronger, I considered that the risk was justifiable and decided to take it."   Taking advantage of around-the-clock daylight the Allied fleet, consisting of the cruisers Attentive and Amiral Aube, the seaplane carrier Nairana, six armed trawlers, and two gunboats, departed on the evening of 30 July.   The Olympia was left at Murmansk; however, Captain Bierer joined Poole on board the yacht Salvator.   The following day four transports escorted by a Russian destroyer and four armed trawlers departed, carrying the bulk of the soldiers including three officers and fifty-one sailors from the Olympia.   A few hours previously the first shots of the campaign were fired at Onega, located about fifty miles to the west of Archangel. Here a small British force crossed the White Sea from the port of Kem aboard the steamship Archangel Michael and succeeded in taking the thirteen Bolshevik defenders completely by surprise.   From Onega it was hoped that Colonel C. J. M. Thornhill and his troops would be able to advance eastward to Oberskaya on the

Archangel-Vologda Railroad and cut the Bolshevik
escape route to the south. But, as Poole reported,
"This force was unable to reach its destination owing
to the severe opposition encountered, but it fought
most gallantly against great odds and eventually
withdrew to Onega after having inflicted severe
casualties on the enemy. It succeeded, however, in
diverting a considerable force from my part and thus
was of considerable assistance to my operations."[5]

At Archangel there was no possibility of repeating
the easy success achieved at Onega as the Bolsheviks
had been warned by telegraph from Murmansk the moment
the British fleet put to sea. Furthermore, the
attackers were hampered by a heavy sea, damp cold,
and clouds. While entering the White Sea in heavy
fog, Poole and Admiral Kemp suffered a major setback
when the Amiral Aube struck an old wreck and was
temporarily disabled. As matters turned out, however,
the vessel was able to free itself after a few hours.
Poole and Kemp, unable in the fog to predict when or
whether the ship would be able to refloat itself,
decided to carry on with the two remaining ships,
the Attentive and the Nairana. On board the yacht
Salvator Captain Bierer of the Olympia and General
Poole witnessed the ensuing sea and air battle for
Mudyug Island.

For a short time it appeared that the mere threat
of force would be sufficient. Apparently intimidated
by the guns of the Attentive, the Bolsheviks signaled
a willingness to surrender unconditionally. However,
before the British were able to land troops the
Bolsheviks reversed themselves. Supposedly the
Attentive mistook the first shell fired by the
defenders "for the bumping of the ship's side against
another piece of ice." Yet, according to Captain
Bierer, it was the Attentive that first opened fire
from a position shrewdly located to the north of the
Bolshevik batteries. Captain Bierer counted about
thirty shots fired by the Attentive, while the
Bolsheviks retaliated with wild shooting--except
for a shell that perforated one of the four funnels
of the British cruiser.[6]

At the same time the British made effective use
of air power, a secret weapon which was then a novelty
in North Russia. Earlier when the Short seaplanes had
held a rehearsal at Murmansk it was observed that the
townspeople were extremely agitated. One woman cried
hysterically that the planes were "devils from Hell,"
and could not be made to understand that the craft
would not harm her. At Mudyug Island the carrier
Nairana launched three seaplanes (piloted by two
Canadians, Lieutenant Dugald MacDonald and Captain

G. H. Simpson; and Major Francis Moller, an Englishman). All the bombs seem to have missed, but the psychological effect of the seaplanes and the gunfire from the <u>Attentive</u> caused the Bolsheviks "to hop it." By 8:00 p.m. the Bolsheviks had fled the island by boat. "The enemy had been working very hard to complete their defences," concluded Poole, "and had our attack been delayed a few weeks longer the capture of the island would have constituted a very serious operation."[7]

In Archangel itself the atmosphere was calm during the morning, but in the afternoon several British seaplanes flew over the city dropping pamphlets and it soon became generally known that the British had seized the harbor's outer defenses. Late in the afternoon the Bolsheviks began a hurried evacuation southward toward Vologda by railroad and by boat toward Kotlas on the Dvina River. As they departed the Bolsheviks sank two icebreakers in the main shipping channel. Early the next morning (2 August 1918), having cleared the Bolshevik mine field, Poole was fortunate enough to find that there was "just sufficient room" between the sunken icebreakers to permit the Allied vessels to pass.[8]

Throughout these events Cole and Consul Maurice Pierce remained out of sight in the American consulate. Fearing their imminent arrest, the two "placed the codes beside an open stove with a bottle of kerosene and a constantly burning candle in preparation for immediate destruction in case of necessity and gave directions that anyone demanding entrance should be detained in conversation at the door." At 11:00 p.m., after Pierce had gone out to observe the evacuation, Cole was arrested by several officers arriving in an automobile. The codes were hurriedly destroyed and Cole was taken to a "modern mansion" where he was held with the British consul and vice consul, together with the French consul and a number of French and British officers. As it turned out, the arrest was not a political act at all, but was motivated by criminal considerations. Those responsible had made off with a Bolshevik safe containing 4,500,000 rubles and the consuls were taken as hostages to ensure the success of the enterprise. The following day at 11:00 a.m. Cole and the others were freed unharmed.[9]

The release came just in time for Cole to witness the landing of General Poole. A few hours before, Chaplin and his fellow conspirators had rounded up the few remaining Bolsheviks and proclaimed the existence of a new government. Seven of the eight cabinet officers, including President Chaikovsky, had formerly

been members of the Constituent Assembly. One of the
first actions of the new government, undertaken "in
the name of a free fatherland and of the Achievements
of the Revolution," was to invite General Poole and
his tiny force of fewer than 1,500 onto Russian soil.
As the troops marched to the government buildings they
were greeted with cheers, whistles, and the waving of
handkerchiefs. Captain Bierer was so overwhelmed by
the demonstration that he recorded: "The people
simply went wild with joy to an extent almost beyond
imagination." However, noted Cole, "it was plain to
be seen that this enthusiasm was confined to certain
classes." Only the middle class and the peasantry,
the two groups that had suffered the most at the hands
of the Bolsheviks, displayed approval. "The working
class," Cole observed, "was patently absent."[10]

Thus, a combination of luck, naval skill, and
what the commander of the _Attentive_ called "sheer
effrontery," had produced a decisive victory without
the loss of a single Allied soldier. The success
seemed to justify Poole's boast to the War Office:
"I occupied Archangel today." Yet, as one participant
pointed out, the easy triumph was not entirely
fortunate as it "gave our commanders an erroneous
judgment of values. The road to Moscow appeared to
be strewn with roses!" More than ever the Bolsheviks
appeared as inept visionaries who were incapable of
offering effective resistance. As General R. G.
Finlayson later noted, the Bolsheviks were mistakenly
dismissed as "a great rabble of men armed with staves,
stones and revolvers, who rush about foaming at the
mouth in search of blood and who are easily turned
and broken by a few well-directed rifle shots."
Ambassador Francis was so confident of victory that
he predicted that the Allies would capture Moscow
"within a month or two." Even the Supreme War
Council subscribed to the myth of Bolshevik impotence,
concluding that "the Bolsheviks had no real power with
which to support their rule. They have entirely
failed to raise an effective army. They remain in
office simply because Russia is too divided to create
any alternative organization with which to supplant
them."[11]

With his polyglot force of fewer than 1,500,
Poole commenced his novel campaign for the conquest of
Russia from the north. Initially the inept resistance
offered by the disorganized Bolsheviks seemed to
justify the contemptuous attitude of Poole. Within
a few days Allied troops were able to advance forty
versts southward toward Vologda along the railroad (a
verst equals .66 of a mile). "Rear guard sniping from
engines and burning bridges have hampered advance,"

reported Poole. American sailors from the <u>Olympia</u>,
apparently suffering from cabin fever, played a daring
role in the early stages of the campaign. Riding a
lame locomotive, Ensign Donald M. Hicks and a dozen
seamen participated in a wild chase after the
retreating Bolsheviks. Two days later Hicks returned
to Archangel in charge of fifty-four young, dirty,
hungry, and frightened Bolshevik prisoners. That the
Bolsheviks, as Poole pointed out, were incapable of
more than rear guard skirmishes was undoubtedly true.
The only surprising development was that the
resistance stiffened appreciably as the Allies neared
Oberskaya, seventy-five miles to the south. To Poole
only one explanation was plausible: the Bolsheviks
were being led by Germans. "This is confirmed," he
reported, "by the finding of trenches dug according
to German methods, unusual accuracy of fire from both
guns and machine guns, tenacity in defence, etc."[12]
    A second major expedition (the Dvina Force) was
organized by Poole to chase the retreating Bolsheviks
on the Dvina River. Poole's goal was the capture
of Kotlas, four hundred miles to the southeast. A
branch of the Trans-Siberian Railroad terminated at
Kotlas and thus the capture of the city would have
theoretically enabled Poole to make contact with the
Czechs. On 6 August a force of about four hundred
French, British, Russians, and Poles departed in
three steamers. As Poole recalled, these troops "were
equipped and despatched under very great difficulties.
We were short of ships as the Bolsheviks had taken all
the best and fastest ones." Furthermore, noted Poole,
"the difficulties of conversing with and administering
these mixed nationalities can readily be imagined."
When Poole inspected the Polish contingent he
discovered, to his shock, that both of the unit's
noncommissioned officers had served in the German
army and both had been wounded fighting against the
Allies on the western front.[13]
    As had been the case on the railroad, progress
at first was amazingly easy. In two days the
Dvina Force advanced 140 miles to Beresnik without
encountering significant opposition. The river route
to Kotlas appeared to be wide open. But at Beresnik,
strategically located near the confluence of the Vaga
River and the Dvina, unexpectedly strong opposition
was encountered. Four Bolshevik gunboats firing
long range naval guns blocked the way. The French
commander of the river expedition was "severely
wounded by rifle shot," and the remaining troops were
pinned down by the Bolsheviks' shelling. Poole then
placed Colonel John Josselyn in command. With the
assistance of two improvised gunboats and the monitor

M25, Josselyn was soon able to drive the Bolsheviks
further up river. Still a number of formidable
problems remained. Supplies had to be shipped almost
200 miles by boat on the swift and unpredictable
Dvina, a river that in its lower reaches was almost
two miles across, but that at other places was so
narrow "that a fisherman could make a cast from one
side to the other." It was a river with a reputation
for never giving up its dead. To haul supplies by
barge, tugboats were necessary and the few that
remained were, according to Poole, "in a bad state
and this renders difficulties for our supply questions
for the river force." Also deficient were the
improvised gunboats which "were too weak to stand the
strain of constant employment and after a few weeks
began to leak badly, suffer from engine troubles and
need constant overhaul. Moreover the decks were too
flimsy to stand the strain of discharge of the guns,
and thus our guns were constantly going out of action
at the critical period."[14]

Even the monitor, reputed to be "a veritable
dreadnought," proved ill-adapted to river fighting
as it was too bulky and deep in draft to maneuver
easily in the swift meandering stream. Nor was the
monitor invulnerable to attack. On 28 August, M25
fought a duel with a Bolshevik artillery battery,
managing to silence it but at a heavy cost of four
dead and seven wounded. As a result of this and
other unhappy encounters with Bolshevik artillery,
Josselyn suggested that tactics of extreme caution
be adopted in the future. In particular, Josselyn
warned commanders to beware of the Bolsheviks' skill
in camouflaging artillery batteries:

> One form of ambush much practiced by
> the enemy was the concealment of batteries
> of light guns and machine guns in the forest
> on the banks of the river and the endeavor
> to draw our Naval Forces on to close range
> of these concealed batteries by retiring
> their gunboats when in action with our Naval
> Forces. These batteries are perfectly
> concealed and aerial reconnaissance can only
> discover them by possibly being able to draw
> them into firing on the reconnoitering
> aeroplane.
> If the Naval Forces get drawn into
> operations ahead of the advance guards of the
> Land Forces very careful watch on the banks
> ahead should be kept, and in particular any
> apparent encouragement by inhabitants on the

banks to continue their pursuing action
should be viewed with suspicion.

For his artillery support Poole had no choice but to
rely on the gunboats, as he found it "most difficult"
to find qualified British personnel to man his
eighteen-pound guns. Forty Polish officers trained
at Murmansk served as the nucleus of Poole's
artillery, but attempts to train Russians as gunners
proved a frustrating experience. "The uneducated
Russian is very hard to teach," Poole lamented.[15]
    Only a minority of the population actually
assisted the Bolsheviks by joining their forces or by
signaling to their gunboats and shore batteries. The
majority of the North Russian peasants pragmatically
straddled the political fence; they had no particular
love for the Bolsheviks, but could stoically put up
with them. General R. G. Finlayson observed that
most of the inhabitants "were more pleased than not
to see us, for we gave the promise of more food and
tobacco, both of which they were beginning to run
short." However, the "only ones who were really
glad" to see the Allies were "the industrious and
the better-to-do peasants" whose surpluses had been
confiscated by the Bolsheviks and distributed to
"their lazy followers who had produced nothing."
The general desire to avoid taking sides was also
demonstrated by the unimpressive progress made in
recruiting troops, as fewer than 1,000 enlisted
during August. In the opinion of Poole, the lack
of volunteers was attributable to "a regrettable
tendency to look to the Allies for food, pay and
protection, thus leaving the Russians themselves
free to indulge in their favourite pastime of
Political intrigue." To Felix Cole the recruiting
disappointments could not have come as a surprise
since, as he had earlier warned the State Department,
"Intervention cannot reckon on active support from
Russians. All the fight is out of Russia." Still
Poole was optimistic that a general mobilization,
which the Chaikovsky government declared under duress
on 20 August, would enable him to raise an army of
10,000 Russians for a spring offensive.[16]
    Political troubles also confounded Poole as he
found that "the Government which had assumed control
about two hours before our arrival here was hopeless
to a degree. It was composed entirely of Left Social
Revolutionaries who in politics and ideas are not far
removed from Bolsheviks." From Poole's perspective
President Chaikovsky and his fellow socialists were
impractical idealists who "were totally incapable of
understanding the necessity of any military

precautions being taken for the safety of the Port.
Any action of this kind they considered as repressive
and as undue interference with the liberties of the
people." Disgusted by the government's "absolute
neglect" of "urgent necessities," Poole arbitrarily
ruled as military governor; he placed the occupied
areas under British martial law and notified
Chaikovsky by letter of his decisions after the fact.
Also highly dissatisfied with the new government was
Captain Chaplin, who had been appointed by Chaikovsky
as commander of the Russian troops.[17] Chaplin had
been under the impression that the cabinet would
represent the business interests of the region and
he was angered when Chaikovsky selected only Socialist
ministers. Having already overthrown one government,
it is hardly surprising that Chaplin began to
contemplate a new coup.

Another complication for Poole was the arrival
at Archangel on 9 August of the Allied ambassadors
from Kandalaksha. At first the diplomats were
preoccupied with locating housing in overcrowded
Archangel. Ambassador Francis was forced to stay on
shipboard for eight days before being able to rent a
three-room apartment. Thereafter, with little else
to occupy their time, the ambassadors devoted much
attention to meddling in military affairs and local
politics. Frequently Chaikovsky and his ministers
sought to outflank Poole by enlisting the support
of the diplomats. Of the socialist ministers an
exasperated Poole wrote: "Past masters of intrigue,
they immediately commenced to play off the Military
against the Diplomatic Representatives. Thus we
have in one small area, the separate interests of
the Government, the Diplomatic Corps and the Military
with a singularly unhappy result. It does not require
a deep study of history to realise the outcome of
continual attempts of civilian interference in
military measures." Yet, according to the reports
of Felix Cole, Poole's dictatorial reign was anything
but popular within the city. Poole was also widely
blamed, a criticism encouraged by Bolshevik agents,
for the failure of the Allies to send food ships.
Cole at least had the good judgment not to remind
the State Department of his earlier warnings that
the anti-Bolshevik leaders were merely "discredited
office holders seeking to regain power," and that,
because the ground for intervention had not been
properly prepared by offering "baksheesh" to the
population, "the North of Russia is nowhere near
as pro-Ally as it might be."[18]

Despite the accumulated problems, Poole remained
optimistic in outlook. "Generally speaking," he

reported on 17 August, "I am quite satisfied with
the results so far attained but progress would be
much quicker if only the reinforcements of Western
European Troops could arrive." The sanguine
Poole estimated that he would capture Kotlas by
20 September and then push on to Viatka during the
winter. To facilitate the advance Poole requested
some Scottish pipers, a brass band, and a battalion
of British garrison troops. "Already," he explained
on 15 August, "I find it very necessary and shall
want it much more when I occupy Vologda, Kotlas,
and Viatka and it is a serious handicap with my
small forces to tie up active men." Based on the
early successes of the expedition and the apparent
ineptitude of the Bolsheviks, Poole's confidence
appeared justified. But even had he received all the
foreign troops and Russian recruits he anticipated,
Poole was becoming more and more overextended with
each advance. As Felix Cole had written:
"Intervention will begin on a small scale but
with each step forward will grow in its demands
for ships, men, money, and materials. . . . Every
foreign invasion that has gone deep into Russia
has been swallowed up. . . . If we intervene,
going further into Russia as we succeed, we shall
be swallowed up." The amateurish nature of the
enterprise deeply shocked realistic observers
such as the British representative in Moscow, Bruce
Lockhart. "We had committed," the incredulous
Lockhart noted in his memoirs, "the unbelievable
folly of landing at Archangel with fewer than twelve
hundred men."[19] Further folly was soon added when
the intervention was expanded following the arrival
at Archangel in early September of the American
reinforcements.

3

The Americans Arrive

Being sent to fight the Bolsheviks came as a complete
surprise to the Americans who composed the 339th
Infantry Regiment. Originally drafted in June 1918
to fight in France, most of the 4,487 men were from
Michigan. In fact, the regiment was commonly
referred to as "Detroit's Own." To fill vacancies
about 500 draftees from Wisconsin were added. Three
smaller units were also assigned to the expedition:
the 310th Engineers, the 337th Field Hospital, and
the 337th Ambulance Company. Approximately half of
the 788 engineers were from Wisconsin; the medical
units were almost entirely staffed by soldiers from
Michigan, except for a few Wisconsin physicians.
Altogether 5,710 Americans were diverted from France
to Archangel.[1]

Unquestionably the troops were inexperienced as
their training had consisted only of a month at Camp
Custer, followed by a second month spent in crossing
the Atlantic. Arriving at Aldershot, England, they
were outfitted by the British with winter equipment,
including snowshoes, fur caps, long woolen coats, and
the Shackleton boot. Colonel George E. Stewart, the
commander of the 339th Infantry, facetiously asked
the British whether they intended to carry out the
"Britishizing" process to its ultimate extent by
issuing him 5,000 monocles. The soldiers' American
rifles were replaced by Russian rifles (manufactured
by Westinghouse), but the men had little confidence
in them as the ammunition frequently jammed and they
were said to be so inaccurate as to shoot around
corners. Moreover, the bayonet was fixed immovably
to the rifle and rapid fire was impossible. Each man
had fired only ten rounds with the rifle on a range
before the 339th departed from Newcastle on 26 August
1918. Even more unsatisfactory than the rifles was
the Shackleton boot, which proved warm, but extremely

slippery and vulnerable to dampness. When Sir Ernest
Shackleton, the explorer and designer of the boot,
later visited Archangel he observed a soldier walking
on a trail wearing ordinary leather ammunition boots
and asked, "Why are you not wearing your snow boots,
my man?" "You see Sir," he replied, "they are all
very well as drawing room slippers but they're no
bloody good outside."[2]

While assembled for life boat drill the troops
learned officially for the first time that their
destination was North Russia. The captain of one
vessel announced that further drills were being
discontinued since the water was so cold that no
one could live in it more than five minutes anyway.
"Wasn't that a dandy," was the reaction of one
American. Another hazard soon appeared as a virulent
strain of influenza broke out on two of the three
British transports. The illness frequently proved
fatal even to young men in good health and it spread
rapidly due to the close quarters on shipboard.
"They stored us in the hold in a dirty place,"
one soldier recorded in his diary. "Crowded like
sardines. 16 to a table and hammocks were issued
to sleep in. We are very crowded at night." Another
diarist noted: "Spanish influenza breaks out; men
begging for medical attention. Insufficient medical
personnel." By mistake practically no medical
supplies had been placed on board the ships, and the
few medicines left over from training at Camp Custer
were soon exhausted. "Congestion was so bad,"
recalled one soldier, "that men with a temperature
of only 101° or 102° were not put into the hospital
but lay in their hammocks or the decks." On board
the Nagoya, characterized as "one of the dirtiest
transports in use on the high seas," one soldier was
"awakened at night by cries of one of the sick men,
who is delirious with Spanish influenza and calling
for his mother."[3]

Therefore, when the men arrived at Archangel
on 4 September the situation was serious, but only
twenty-five ill Americans could be accommodated by
the British 53rd Stationary Hospital. Under the
direction of Major Jonas R. Longley of Fond du Lac,
Wisconsin, who was himself "nearly dead of the
disease," an American hospital was established with
supplies and nurses furnished by the American Red
Cross and the Russian Red Cross. "The patients had
no beds," recalled one medic. "They lay on stretchers
without mattresses or pillows, lying in their O.D.
uniforms, with only a simple blanket for covering.
The place was a bedlam of sinister sounds of rasping,
stertorous breathing, coughings, hackings, moans and

incoherent cries." In September 378 Americans were
afflicted by influenza and eventually seventy-two died
of the disease or the resulting pneumonia. Lieutenant
Marcus T. Casey of New Richmond, Wisconsin, a law
student at the University of Wisconsin, was one of
the first to succumb to the disease. At Archangel,
Casey received an elaborate military funeral that was
heavily attended by the well-to-do. However, as had
been the case when General Poole landed a month and a
half before, the laboring classes were conspicuously
absent.[4]

For a time the local manufacturers of coffins were
unable to keep up with the demand, and the churches
worked overtime conducting funerals for the American
and Russian victims. One American medical officer
observed that the Orthodox priests routinely used the
same yellow robe to cover all corpses and during the
funeral chants each member of the congregation kissed
the same spot on an icon held by the priest. "It is
their belief," he noted, "that during a religious
service it is impossible to contract disease."
The high death rate may have been aggravated by the
general lack of sanitation at Archangel. The sewer
system consisted merely of ditches under the sidewalks
that emptied into large, frequently overflowing
cesspools. The barracks where the sick men were
confined were unventilated, had filthy latrines,
and were surrounded by grounds contaminated by sewage
and the excrement of dogs and horses. "This is some
city," reported Lieutenant Charles Ryan to Professor
John R. Commons of the University of Wisconsin. "It
can be smelled for quite a distance. Among his other
crimes, Peter the Great was responsible for this
place." Another arriving soldier recorded, "Never
did I strike such a fine set of assorted odors." And
with only slight exaggeration the American Sentinel,
a house organ printed at Archangel for the American
troops, reported: "Up here in this tough town there
are 269,831 inhabitants, of which 61,329 are human
beings and 208,502 are dogs. The wind whistles
across the Dvina River like the Twentieth Century
Limited passing Podunk."[5]

Under normal circumstances the cesspools were
periodically emptied and their contents carted off
to the swamps and tundra. But as Major Longley
pointed out: "Due to the disorganization resultant
from war conditions, the labor necessary to effect
this had been lacking, the cess pits had overflowed,
flush latrines had become plugged and human excreta
was conspicuous and abundant both inside and outside
of buildings." Under the supervision of the 310th
Engineers the odoriferous job of emptying and cleaning

latrines and cess pits was begun. Bathhouses,
incinerators, and a delousing station (the "cooty
mill") were constructed. As a result, noted Longley,
"before winter made outdoor work impossible, the
situation had been greatly improved."[6]

The moral climate of North Russia left much to be
desired also. "Venereal Disease is very prevalent,"
warned a British pamphlet. "To avoid this KEEP
STRAIGHT." Soldiers were especially instructed by
Poole to avoid Archangel's notorious Cafe de Paris
as "women of easy virtue habitually visit the cafe
for the purposes of their profession." However,
despite the issuance of prophylactic kits to all
ranks, the American hospital at Archangel was kept
busy treating a mounting number of cases of venereal
disease. By the end of March 1919, the hospital had
tallied 54 cases of syphilis and 129 of gonorrhea.
The problem did not abate until the American
Commander, Colonel George Stewart, began, in February
1919, to court-martial soldiers for contracting
venereal disease (ninety-five convictions) and for
failure to take venereal prophylaxis (fifty-three
convictions). A penalty of three months' confinement
at hard labor and the forfeiture of two-thirds pay
for the same period was routinely imposed.[7]

Company C of the engineers received the most
pleasant duties of any of the new arrivals. In the
early morning hours of 6 September Captain Chaplin
and thirty confederates arrested President Chaikovsky
and six of his eight ministers. The captives were
then summarily deported to the Solovetski Monastery
located on Solovetski Island in the White Sea, a
thirty-hour voyage from Archangel. Francis and his
colleagues were horrified ("The hell you say!" was
the ambassador's reaction) because they saw that the
kidnapping would surely be blamed on the unpopular
Poole and the newly arrived Americans. To his face
Francis told Chaplin that his action was "the most
flagrant usurpation of power I ever knew." The coup
roused the normally apathetic population into a very
effective general strike demonstrating their sympathy
with Chaikovsky. In response to an appeal from Poole,
American soldiers were detailed to operate the
Archangel power plant and waterworks, run a sawmill,
and operate the local streetcar system. One problem
with the latter occupation was that the Americans
neither knew the language nor understood the value of
the money presented by the passengers. Therefore, as
one participant recalled, "No change was ever given.
The motorman would go down the street hollering
Michigan Avenue, Woodward Avenue and other streets
in Detroit." After two days the strike ended as a

British warship returned the president and his
ministers to Archangel. Chaplin, defended by Poole,
escaped serious punishment for his part in the affair,
merely being sent to the front rather than being put
on trial. Although Chaikovsky was restored to power
the entire affair demonstrated how dependent the weak
government was upon the Allies. As a result of the
coup the government suffered a blow to its prestige
from which it never really recovered.[8]

In the meantime General Poole sent about half the
American troops southward in boxcars toward Vologda.
Their immediate destination was Oberskaya, seventy
miles away, a town that the French had seized on
4 September while inflicting heavy casualties on the
Bolsheviks and taking 200 prisoners. However, further
progress proved agonizingly slow as the Bolsheviks
took advantage of the swampy terrain. As summed up
by Poole: "The country consisting of practically
nothing but forest and bog presents the most
extraordinary difficulties. This renders any attempt
at a turning movement both difficult and slow. For a
detachment to have to wade waist deep in bog even on
patrol work is almost a daily occurrence." Between
Archangel and Vologda (425 miles to the south) there
were 262 bridges and, noted Poole, "as my forces stand
at present I shall be held up at every bridge, each of
which takes some days to repair."[9]

At first the Americans' inexperience was
painfully evident. Two columns of American troops
naively held roll call along the railroad track when
"an excited little French officer popped out of his
dugout and pointed at the shell holes in the ground."
Fortunately, the troops were dispersed before the
Bolsheviks opened artillery fire from what appeared
to be a sawmill smokestack three miles down the track.
In fact, the "smokestack" was a naval gun mounted on
a Bolshevik armored train. "Suddenly it flashed,"
recalled one observer. "Then came the distant boom.
Came then the twist-whistling shell that passed over
us and showered shrapnel near the trenches where lay
our reserves."[10] Through good luck and inaccurate
Bolshevik marksmanship the amateur soldiers escaped
injury.

After three weeks of training the Americans
were considered sufficiently prepared to attempt
an offensive against the Bolshevik armored train,
located ten miles to the south at verst marker 455.
Now the British had assembled their own armored train
equipped with an eighteen-pound artillery piece, one
75-mm cannon, and two 3.3-inch naval guns. The large
guns were mounted on coal cars protected by sandbags
and defended by a carload of soldiers armed with

Vickers machine guns and Lewis automatic rifles.
On the afternoon of 28 September, one company of
Americans tried to outflank the Bolsheviks by
marching through what one officer called "an almost
impossible swampy bog. . . . The men and their
equipment were often waist deep in the mire."
Predictably the men became hopelessly lost in
the dark and failed to reach their objective.
The next morning the remaining Americans, assisted
by the French, started their assault. But soon the
Bolsheviks counterattacked, taking back all the
ground they had lost. Contributing to the fiasco
were malfunctioning machine guns and inept shelling
by the Allied armored train, which mistakenly hit a
bridge held by American troops.[11]

Two weeks later the Americans attempted a similar
attack. The plan was for a party of engineers to slip
to the rear of verst 455, destroy the track, and trap
the Bolshevik armored train. Once again the strategy
miscarried as the engineers were unable to get behind
the Bolsheviks. Therefore, when the Allies attacked
at 6:40 a.m. on 14 October the Bolsheviks simply
withdrew their armored train and troop train to the
rear, destroyed another bridge, and surrendered three
versts (about two miles) of track. Sent to the front
without their barracks bags or tents, the infantrymen
found themselves drenched from rain and half-frozen
from camping on the tundra. One private noted in his
diary: "Spent the worst night ever, no blankets, no
fires, and soaking wet, could not even sit down. I
have not had any sleep since Saturday night. Nothing
happened, however, but rain and mosquitoes. I am just
covered with bites. . . . We are not as well equipped
as were our soldiers in the Spanish War." Another
soldier recalled that when the Bolsheviks opened fire
with machine guns and artillery "our boys had to go
right in the swamps up to their knees in water and
mud." And when one American was shot through the
head by a sniper he was buried in what one soldier
characterized as "a most dismal spot, a clearing in
the woods a mile or so behind the front lines. The
place was swampy and water stood in the grave; the
dank forest rose like a smoldering wall to encircle
us." The tenacity of the Russian resistance and the
accuracy of their fire again led Poole to the mistaken
conclusion that German officers were masterminding
the defense.[12]

Poole's operations on the Dvina during September
were somewhat more successful. Three days after their
arrival at Archangel, four companies of Americans were
loaded onto coal barges, which reminded one passenger
of Noah's Ark. After a five-day journey, towed by a

wood-burning tugboat, they reached their initial
destination of Beresnik 140 miles upstream. On the
second day a soldier from Wyandotte, Michigan died of
influenza and the corpse was placed in an improvised
coffin. Thereupon, as described by Private Edwin
Arkins, "Blood from underneath coffin trickles across
floor of barge while we eat our hard tack and black
tea. Sleep on our blankets on bottom of barge; very
damp. Our faces and uniforms are black with moist
coal dust." By the time the barges reached Beresnik,
without encountering opposition, two more soldiers
had died. "On the barge there was no heat, and no
beds," recalled one participant. "The men died on
their blankets on the bare floor."[13]

After two days of training at Beresnik one
company of Americans was ordered to advance up the
Dvina on foot. At first the amateur soldiers met
only token opposition from a few snipers, which was
fortunate as their lack of experience was painfully
evident. In particular the troops were inclined to
fire at anything that moved. In occupying a nearby
village Arkins recorded: "A little excitement when
scouting party mistakes runaway horse for enemy
attack. Several shots fired. No one hurt." And a
few days later a patrol probing a Bolshevik position
returned practically empty-handed. "All we bring
back," noted Arkins, "is dead chicken after firing
fusillade in error."[14]

From his base at Beresnik, Poole's strategy was
to launch a two-pronged offensive against Kotlas.
His main attack was directed at the Bolshevik flotilla
on the Dvina. On land the brunt of the task fell to
the Royal Scots, who advanced on both sides of the
river via primitive mud-choked roads. The less
experienced Americans were ordered to advance up the
west bank of the Dvina. "The movements of these
troops," noted Poole, "were seriously impeded by the
boggy nature of the roads and their guns had to be
brought up by barge eventually. British and Russian
aeroplanes and seaplanes have been continually flying
observing and bombing the enemy." The plan counted
upon the British monitor and supporting ships being
able to defeat the gunboats of the Bolsheviks. As
Poole optimistically wrote:

I hope that with this force I may be
able to bring off a coup which will sink or
capture the enemy fleet annihilate the force
and capture the guns. If I can bring this
off successfully at an early date I do not
think I shall meet with any more serious
opposition before reaching Kotlas which I

am reckoning on being able to occupy by
September 20th and push on towards Viatka
during the winter.[15]

A second feature of Poole's strategy was to advance
up the Vaga River with the objective of outflanking
the Bolsheviks by means of a turning movement from
the west.

The Vaga phase of the operation went exceptionally
well. Preceded by two gunboats, a company of
Americans in barges advanced toward the town of
Shenkursk forty miles upstream. In just two days the
Americans, meeting only a few snipers, were able to
occupy their objective. However, the offensive on
the Dvina met determined resistance as Poole found
the Bolsheviks to be "in considerable force on both
banks of the river, and in considerable force also
in ships." The fighting was especially fierce for
Chamova, located on the west bank of the Dvina
fifteen miles from Beresnik. Here the Bolshevik
gunboat Moochovga was surprised in the fog by M25 and
sunk by a barrage of 7.5-mm shells. However, reported
Poole, the Allied flotilla was shelled by concealed
shore batteries "and our ships were compelled to
withdraw again to the mouth of the Vaga." By dawn on
15 September the Royal Scots succeeded in occupying
the town where they captured several three-inch guns,
some gun carriages, an automobile, and a few horses.
The next day a number of the Royal Scots fell victim
to a ruse when a Bolshevik steamer brazenly docked at
Chamova. Mistaking the vessel for an Allied supply
ship, several of the Scots unwisely approached
unarmed, whereupon the Red sailors proceeded to kill
three of their adversaries using small axes, which
Russians customarily wore in their belts. At this
point M25 arrived and, according to the diary of
Henry Katz, "planted a shell in the Bolshevik boat
and set it on fire. Several loud explosions took
place and the boat sank." Shellfire from M25 also
damaged the Bolshevik gunboat Bogatyr which was later
reported to have sunk.[16]

Meanwhile, a day's march behind, two companies
of green American infantrymen occupied the positions
vacated by the Scots. "It was a bad march through
mud and swamp," Lieutenant Glen Weeks noted in his
diary. "We were all homesick." Twenty-five miles
further the Americans, supported by White Russian
artillery, drove the Bolsheviks out of Seltso, taking
twenty-three prisoners, but at the cost of four
killed, eight wounded, and one missing. "The sight
of that first casualty I'll never forget," recorded
Edwin Arkins. "The lower part of face a bloody mass;

the eye lids swollen and blue and the head resting on
the inside of the upturned helmet." One of the dead
was Corporal Morris Foley who was hit in the face by
machine-gun fire. Among the troops the story was told
that Foley "fell and took off his pack and unrolled
his blanket and laid down before he died." Later
three Bolshevik gunboats shelled the town before
being driven off by artillery.[17]

By the end of September Poole had advanced
fifty miles and in the process the Allies sank four
enemy ships and two barges, killed an estimated 200
Bolsheviks, and captured 100 prisoners in addition
to assorted guns, ammunition, horses, carts, and
uniforms. However, the Bolsheviks then blocked the
river by sinking two lines of sand-filled barges which
were supplemented by mine fields. Always stressing
the positive, Poole praised his small forces for
having "carried out its operations under most
difficult conditions to my entire satisfaction."
Yet the hard fact was that Poole's offensive had
stalled, having advanced only about half way toward
its objective of Kotlas. As Poole explained the
situation: "The approach of winter, lateness in
arrival of stores, and shortages of tugs to tow the
barges of supplies up the river have decided me not
to attempt a further advance toward Kotlas until the
spring."[18]

How, two months after President Wilson's aide-
mémoire of 17 July 1918 (which restricted American
troops in Russia to guarding military stores), did
two American battalions come to find themselves
engaged in a shooting war against the Bolsheviks deep
in the interior of North Russia? In the opinion of
the American soldiers the responsibility for their
predicament lay squarely in the lap of General Poole.
As summed up by Captain Robert P. Boyd, Poole naively
thought that his name alone would work wonders, and
that the Russians would do the fighting while the
Allies guarded the supplies. But, explained Boyd,
the result was that "the Russians stole the supplies
and we did the fighting." Undoubtedly Poole richly
deserved criticism for his general egotism and
arrogance, for his establishment of a military
dictatorship at a time when Wilson was stressing
self-determination, and for his total underestimation
of the Bolsheviks--he actually told his second in
command, General Edmund Ironside, that the Bolsheviks,
lacking officers and knowledge of warfare, would soon
be in a hopeless position and unable to stand up to
the avalanche that would bury them. However, the
general's disregard of the inept and feuding Russian
politicians at Archangel was fully justified in his

eyes inasmuch as Poole himself viewed the expedition
as a wild gamble whose success depended upon ruthless
efficiency rather than on a legalistic concern for
democracy.[19] Moreover, there is considerable doubt
that Poole was even aware of the restrictions imposed
by Wilson concerning the use of American troops until
four weeks after the 339th Infantry landed at
Archangel.

When Poole occupied Archangel on 2 August he
operated under a vague set of orders that had been
drafted on 18 May 1918 by General Henry Wilson,
commander of the Imperial General Staff. Since at
that time it was unknown whether the United States
would even agree to participate in the intervention,
Poole was told to organize the Czechs, White
Russians, and whatever Allied forces arrived in North
Russia. After the capture of Archangel, Poole was
provided with a new set of instructions on 10 August,
necessitated by the failure of the Czechs to penetrate
to the northern ports. Once again Poole was told to
make contact with the Czechs "and to secure with their
assistance, control of the Archangel-Vologda-
Ekaterinburg Railway and the river and railway line
communications between Viatka and Archangel." At the
same time Poole was to recruit armed forces among the
Russian population, support "any administration which
may be friendly to the Allies," provide relief to
the civil population, and engage in "judicious
propaganda." Already, however, the War Office was
having second thoughts about the practicality of
linking forces with the Czechs, and Poole was told
that if he were unable to establish contact with
the Czechs he should concentrate his efforts upon
recruiting troops and upon organizing the defense of
Archangel. Finally Poole was informed that no more
troops could be sent, beyond the American battalions
en route, but his instructions failed to mention any
restrictions upon the use of the Americans.[20]

Conceivably Poole could have been enlightened by
the American ambassador David R. Francis, who had
been present at Archangel since 9 August. Francis,
despite difficulties in communicating with Washington,
was not ignorant of the fact that Wilson had limited
the role of American troops in Russia to guarding
military stores. On 23 August Francis acknowledged
receipt of a State Department cable that paraphrased
Wilson's policy on the use of American troops. The
president's 17 July aide-mémoire, however, was worded
in such abstract terms that it was open to numerous
interpretations. As an interventionist, Francis
chose to interpret liberally Wilson's policy as
sanctioning the pursuit of American supplies to

wherever the Bolsheviks had shipped them, including
Moscow and Petrograd. And in his communications
with the State Department, Francis made no attempt
to conceal his views. A week before the arrival of
the 339th Infantry, Francis reported that he would
"encourage American troops if and when landed to
proceed to such points in the interior as Kotlas,
Sukhona, and Vologda" in order to reclaim military
supplies "which the Soviet Government, in violation
of its promises and agreements transferred from
Archangel." In addition, Francis informed the State
Department, he would "encourage American troops to
obey the commands of General Poole in his effort to
effect a junction with the Czechoslovaks." Francis
did not justify assisting the Czechs as a step to
protect war stores, but maintained that the actions
would aid in suppressing the "menace" of bolshevism
which was "virtually inspired and directed from
Germany." Because Francis mailed his dispatch it was
not received in Washington until 15 October. However,
in a cable sent the day before the arrival of the
339th Infantry at Archangel, Francis plainly stated
that he would not object if General Poole asked
permission to send Americans into the interior.[21]

Although Francis was seriously misinterpreting
the policy of his own government, three weeks passed
before Washington raised objections. The delay was
especially unfortunate for the men of the 339th
Infantry since during the first three weeks of
September they were being deployed by General Poole
into the North Russian interior. Gradually, however,
unmistakable evidence accumulated that Poole was
misusing the American troops. First, General Tasker
Bliss, the American representative on the Supreme War
Council at Versailles, took a firm stand against a
British request to send five more American battalions
to North Russia. Such a suggestion made Bliss
suspicious that the British had "bitten off more than
they can chew." Bliss was informed of the British
desire for reinforcements by Major Francis Riggs, who
arrived at Paris on 7 September. His theme, which
struck Bliss as wild talk, was that the additional
troops would enable Poole to "force himself to parts
of Russia where he will secure volunteers and where
he can then get into contact with the Czechs and as
a result of it they will practically conquer Western
Russia and re-establish a front against the Germans."
Most incredible to Bliss was the news that Poole had
supposedly been promised 10,000 American troops. From
what source Poole could have gotten such a figure "I
cannot conceive," Bliss wrote Francis. In his view,
stated Bliss, the Wilson administration had only

agreed to intervene at Murmansk and Archangel "with very great reluctance and that its sole idea was that the American troops sent there were for the sole purpose of guarding certain military stores supposed to have been left at those ports, and of preventing the Germans from occupying those ports." It was not his business to question Wilson's decision, wrote Bliss, "and I accept it loyally."[22]

Based upon the slim information coming from Russia, President Wilson became increasingly irate about Poole's direction of the campaign. As early as 5 September Wilson complained to Lansing that Poole was disregarding his wishes by seeking to bring the Czechs westward (for use against the Bolsheviks) instead of evacuating them to the east. Wilson's disillusionment deepened as he received reports of Poole's "high-handed" conduct in dealing with the Chaikovsky government. By 18 September Wilson asked Lansing to prepare a note reiterating his opposition to any scheme for reforming the eastern front since such an idea was "absolutely impracticable from a military point of view and unwise as a matter of political action." More than ever Wilson was convinced that Poole's predictions were nothing more than wishful thinking. The large number of Russian volunteers counted upon by Poole had not materialized and, wrote Wilson, "the situation is not at all what it was anticipated that it would develop into."[23]

Finally, on 26 September, three weeks after the arrival of the 339th Infantry, Lansing formally clarified American policy. Using an outline provided by the president, Lansing notified Francis "that all military effort in northern Russia [must] be given up except the guarding of the ports themselves and as much of the country round them as may develop threatening conditions." But Francis was not censured for encouraging Poole; rather, in the same communication, he was told: "The course which you have followed is most earnestly commended. It has the entire admiration of the President who has characterized it as being thoroughly American. I highly approve of your actions. They have been consistent and have been guided by a very sound judgment exercised under the most trying and difficult circumstances." Presumably Lansing's praise was meant to apply to the ambassador's encouragement of an independent Russian government at Archangel rather than to his support of Poole.[24]

Six days later (2 October 1918), Poole had "a long and very friendly talk" with Francis in which the ambassador produced Lansing's cable and explained that the American troops were to be used only for

defensive purposes. "The Ambassador says in
confidence," Poole reported, "that he will take
a very liberal view of the latter part of this
order, but he is a man so easily influenced by the
last speaker, that it may easily raise an awkward
situation and hamper us in any operations as out
of 5 allied battalions here, 3 are American." This
setback did cause Poole to modify his plans by
relegating the American battalions to serve as base
and supply troops. "They cannot be taken into account
as troops destined for any further fighting," Poole
concluded. To replace the Americans Poole urged the
War Office to transfer from Murmansk four British
battalions as well as three British artillery
batteries. With the addition of these forces Poole
envisaged a winter campaign against Vologda along
the railroad. "If we succeed in reaching Vologda,"
he predicted, "we may well open up line to Viatka."[25]

By now only Poole retained enthusiasm for an
expansion of the conflict. At Versailles General
Bliss reiterated the American opposition to sending
reinforcements to Russia. In London, General Henry
Wilson backed away from Poole's grandiose plans and
told General Ironside on his departure for Archangel:
"Your business in North Russia is to hold the fort
until the local Russians can take the field."
Moreover, the military situation on the western front
was improving to the point where a campaign for "the
restoration of Russia. . . to enable the Russians to
again take the field. . . by the side of the Allies"
(the War Office's 10 August instructions to Poole) no
longer seemed necessary or feasible. To the surprise
of Ironside, Poole decided to present his case in
person to the War Office. Taking advantage of the
return of H.M.S. <u>Attentive</u> to England, Poole left
Archangel on 14 October for what was planned as a
short leave of thirty days. While Poole was on the
water the War Office rejected his proposal citing
the opposition of the Wilson administration as well
as material and logistic difficulties. On his arrival
in London Poole found that not only his plan had been
turned down but that he was being replaced by the
thirty-eight-year-old Ironside. The change in command
meant also a major change in strategy, as Ironside was
instructed that his operations were to be "limited to
the defensive and to the training of the Russians."[26]

4

The Mission of General Ironside

To replace the unpopular Poole, General Henry Wilson selected a thirty-eight-year-old career officer with an unusual name--but one which befitted his profession--General William Edmund Ironside. Besides his distinctive name, Ironside was noted for his immense size; he stood six feet four inches tall and weighed well over 200 pounds. On very short notice he was selected to go to Russia. On 19 September he was still commander of an infantry brigade in France; twelve days later he arrived at Archangel on the S.S. Stephen, a vessel which also carried the nearly 500 members of the badly needed 16th Brigade of the Canadian Field Artillery. An expert linguist, Ironside already possessed a fluent command of the Russian language, but he frankly admitted, "I knew nothing of the northern region. Archangel was to me but a legend of Peter the Great and Richard Chancellor." Likewise, he found the Russian officers on the scene to be unfamiliar with the techniques of river and forest fighting as they "all, before the war, looked upon Archangel and the Northern Region as a horrible place of exile." Undaunted, Ironside found a reliable source of military advice in "the old and well-tried textbook, 'Small Wars,' which was found an infallible guide."[1]

The new commander was a man of great energy and ambition, qualities which Poole also had possessed to a high degree. However, Ironside possessed several characteristics that his predecessor lacked. As a former staff officer he was well equipped to reorganize Poole's tangled administrative structure. Another of his attributes was a generous supply of humility that enabled Ironside philosophically to accept the inevitable nicknames that were applied to him, such as "Tiny," "Big Bill," or "Tin Ribs." He also made a practice of frequently and informally

mingling with soldiers and demonstrating his concern
for their well-being by candidly inquiring about
their needs. Colonel Stewart recalled an occasion
in November when Ironside questioned a group of
American soldiers about the number of letters each
had received during the previous month. The first
answered: "'Twenty-two, Sir'. Another replied in
answer to the same query, 'Thirty-four, Sir,' and a
third replied, 'Sixty-two, Sir.' The General said,
'Never heard of such a thing, why I have been here
two months and I have not yet gotten a letter from
my family.' At which there was a howl of mirth and
we moved on."[2]

Probably the most visible difference between
the two British generals was that Ironside, in
contrast to the tactless Poole, possessed considerable
political ability. Indeed, the necessity of dealing
with the Allied ambassadors, the Chaikovsky
government, and a polyglot army required a first-rate
politician. In this respect Ironside was a great
success. As Ambassador Francis put it, "General
Ironsides [sic] seems to have impressed everybody
favorably." President Chaikovsky told Francis that
he was very pleased by the general's respectful
attitude toward his government. Even the American
soldiers, who were universally critical of the
British officer corps, respected their new commander.
John Cudahy remembered Ironside as "a great tower of
a man, the very embodiment of soldierly force and
resolution." Another American characterized him as
"a man and a soldier, par excellence." As a good
politician, Ironside carefully concealed from the
Americans his low opinion of their fighting ability
and his conviction that the British army and its
methods were far superior to those of the other
Allies. Likewise, Ironside was tactful enough not
to mention his real opinion of President Chaikovsky
and his Socialist-Revolutionary party. In fact,
he considered the president to be "an old plotter"
who "was living quietly in the past," and the
representative of a party that had "no vigorous
plan to put into effect." In short, Ironside soon
came to share the views earlier expressed by Felix
Cole in regard to the anti-Bolshevik intellectuals:
"Their place is around the steaming samovar, not in
the halls of government. Their invitation to enter
Russia is not an invitation from the Russian people.
They misjudge the temper of the Russian people to-day
as badly as they did a year ago."[3] Finally, his
reputation as a diplomat not withstanding, Ironside
could be even more hardboiled and intimidating than
General Poole.

Certainly it took many months for the new
commander to become acquainted with the personalities
involved and to take stock of the troops at his
disposal. For the time being, however, Ironside was
unable to make a personal inspection of his far-flung
forces since he found the country to be "a sea of
impassable mud," which made travel by airplane risky.[4]
At the same time, ice floes on the Dvina ruled out the
use of seaplanes and barges. In fact the worsening
weather was a blessing in disguise as it provided a
lull in the fighting, which lasted for much of the
month of October.

On the railroad front the emphasis was now upon
preparing a strong defensive position. First of all,
the front line at verst 455 was strongly fortified
with barbed wire entanglements (constructed from
40,000 rolls of wire found in Archangel), and these
were supplemented by 316 shellproof blockhouses, 273
machine gun emplacements, and 167 infantry outposts.
One of the most tedious and back-breaking jobs was
constructing blockhouses and clearing lanes of fire
through the dense timber. In the immediate vicinity
of the blockhouses only underbrush was cleared.
Ironside insisted that the blockhouses must be
constructed in forest cover so as to be concealed
from enemy artillery. "In the open," he explained,
"a blockhouse merely becomes a deathtrap." According
to an American observer the defense was very
skillfully prepared, the blockhouses being "well
located for the protection of the flanks and
approaches, giving mutual support by means of
lanes of fire cut through the timber." The base
of operations was located nine versts to the rear.
It consisted of several barracks, used primarily
for medical purposes and Y.M.C.A. work, several
blockhouses, and a high observation tower. Compared
with the housing facilities available elsewhere in
North Russia the troops of the railroad enjoyed
deluxe accommodations in converted railroad cars.
The engineers insulated the walls with sawdust, and
they installed bunks and stoves. Further to the rear
at Oberskaya, where the Royal Air Force maintained a
flying field, the train that housed the officers was
equipped with steam heat supplied by an old engine
and at dusk an electric light began operation. As
summed up by a visiting Canadian, "All in all, it
is about as close to the Ritz as we are likely to
get out here."[5] On the Bolshevik side similar winter
preparations were undertaken as revealed by the sound
of axes ringing across no man's land. With so much
energy being spent on defense the fighting was

confined to an occasional clash of patrols or
exchange of artillery fire.

The month of October on the Dvina front was
also relatively uneventful as the troops worked at
patrolling, drilling, holding target practice, and,
when it was not raining, building fortifications.
Shenkursk, the base for the American troops on the
Vaga River, was a solidly constructed town of about
3,000, featuring brick and frame buildings, a
monastery, and several churches. Ralph Albertson,
a Y.M.C.A. worker at Shenkursk, described the place
as "something of an educational center and summer
resort. . . . There were many comfortable houses
here, some mansions, some interesting people, a most
comfortable place to spend the winter." And it was
generally believed by the troops at Shenkursk that
the worst was over, that they were going into winter
quarters and that fighting would be suspended for the
duration of the winter. In his diary Lieutenant Glen
Weeks noted that much of his time was occupied with
writing letters and opening mail, having his teeth
cleaned, and shooting three wild turkeys which were
served with an excellent peach pie. Other delicacies
available in the vicinity included wild ducks, geese,
partridge, and rabbit, as well as fish which could be
easily caught after having been stunned with a hand
grenade.[6]

Accommodations at Shenkursk and its outpost of
Ust Padenga, eighteen miles upstream, were fairly
adequate. Typically the troops were billeted in
solidly constructed Russian homes, usually in the
summer section of the house, which consisted of one
large room equipped with single windows. The Russian
family occupied the winter quarters, which were better
insulated with thicker walls and double windows.
Each house displayed an icon near the entrance, and,
therefore, much bowing and genuflecting was required
when coming and going. Many of the Americans found
the constant crossing (after and before meals, upon
taking a bath, entering or leaving a home, or shaking
hands) to be a curious but tedious custom. Heat for
the home was provided by a large wood-burning brick
stove. During the cold months it was common for the
occupants to sleep near or on the stove. When the
fire had died down to coals food was cooked in pots
of earthenware crockery and customarily the family
then ate from the same bowl using wooden spoons.[7]

During periods of intense cold, chickens, dogs,
and even sheep and ponies were permitted to sleep
near the stove. Needless to say, the circumstances
were ideal for the flourishing of vermin. "I soon
learned not to lean on the walls," recalled one pilot,

"as the packing between the logs was full of bugs."
Invariably the soldiers found themselves infested
with lice. The standard procedure for coping with
these pests was to locate the lice with the use of
wood or bone combs. "When found," recalled Hugh
McPhail, "the louse would be placed on a thumbnail
and the other thumbnail would be used to crack the
louse with a decided plopping noise." To relieve
boredom, races between giant lice known as Catholic
seam squirrels (so named because of black crosses on
their backs) were occasionally staged across a table.
The pests were completely disrespectful of rank; even
Ambassador Francis had problems, and his servant
Philip Jordan urgently requested from Mrs. Francis
"two large boxes of gitzs best roach powder or the
best kind. I would appreciate this Very much. also
three boxes rough on rats or the best. they crawl
all over me at night. None to be had in Russia."[8]
    Even frequent bathing in saunas, a standard
feature of peasant homes, failed to dislodge all the
vermin. Within the sauna there were usually three
levels, with the most intense heat and steam being
experienced on the higher platforms. Only the
Russians were able to tolerate the upper levels.
"An American would make his will and call the
undertaker before following suit," noted one soldier.
Despite the practice of steam bathing in the winter
and river bathing in the summer, the troops were
acutely aware of a persistent olfactory affront.
The unique smell of Russia appeared to be a blend
of sweat, sewage, manure, incense, and fish oil
soap. As an anonymous soldier's verse indelicately
expressed it: "It's the land of the cootie and
bed-bug,/ the herring and mud-colored crow./ My
strongest impression of Russia/ gets into my head
through my nose./ It's the land of the infernal
odor,/ the land of the national smell./ The average
American soldier/ would rather be quartered in hell."
Still the troops became so accustomed to the Russian
odor that, after leaving the country, they realized
that something was different, "and it was some time
before a clever Yank thought of the reason."[9]
    Probably the most bitter complaints were reserved
for the British field ration. It consisted primarily
of bully beef (a kind of corned beef from Argentina),
M[eat] and V[egetable] mixture (mainly vegetables and
a glob of fat), dehydrated vegetables, ration
biscuits, black tea, tinned butter (mostly liquid
grease), and jam. Unaccustomed to tea, the American
troops greatly missed coffee; they found the biscuits
(four inches long, two inches wide, and a quarter of
an inch thick) almost impossible to break or soften;

and the jam, consisting of rhubarb and ginger, often concealed a pellet of lead that could break the teeth of the unwary. Equally unpopular were the dehydrated vegetables. "These were just impossible," recalled Hugh McPhail. "Even after a good two-or three-day soak in warm water, the vegetables were as unpalatable-looking and as tough to eat as they looked." Captain Joel R. Moore recalled an occasion when the menu featured "grass stew," which was concocted from dehydrated vegetables, and one soldier gave his portion to a Russian woman. "She tasted it," recorded Moore, "and then threw it on some hay before the cow. The cow refused to eat either the 'grass stew' or the hay." Then there was what one pilot characterized as "a revolting food I have not encountered elsewhere--tinned kidneys--which were apparently made by soaking balls of sawdust in a particularly nasty gravy."[10]

Nevertheless, the cooks showed great ingenuity in disguising the British rations and with supplementing meals with local supplies of bread, eggs, and potatoes, as well as sausage and wieners, which it was suspected were stuffed largely with horse and dog meat. "Where," inquired a puzzled corporal, "is that half million dogs that were in Archangel when we landed last September?" When two Americans were served "hasenpfeffer" by the French they observed that a long feline tail decorated the ladle. "Then we remembered the Frenchies throwing their bayonets at cats on the street with great accuracy. We didn't eat seconds." Still, at least on special occasions, the food was better than usual. The Thanksgiving menu of "Battling Company 'I'" began with a shot of rum ("Hit 'Em Hard"), and it also included such international specialties as "Beef ala Rusky," "Roast Beef ala Finish," "Kartophile ala Bolshevik," "Sauerkraut ala Berlin," "Tart ala Peach et Apricot," "Doughnuts--don't eat the center," "coffee au Lait," "Tobacco ala Bull Durham," and "Cigars ala Etats Uni."[11]

If the winter quarters lacked all the comforts of home, they at least provided the Allied troops with relative safety once the initial fighting was over. The general sense of well-being and security seemed further justified by the Allies' control of the skies which, at least in theory, should have given ample warning of possible Bolshevik attacks. Initially, however, aviation played only a minor role in the campaign as it took several months for the Royal Air Force to develop flying facilities and to train pilots to cope with flying in arctic conditions. Originally General Poole's expedition was supplied with only

eight DH-4 biplanes. At Archangel, however, the
Allies were fortunate enough to discover, among the
supplies previously sent to Russia, sufficient RE-8s,
Nieuport 17s, and Sopwith 1 1/2 Strutters to form
two squadrons. To fly this improvised collection of
aircraft, thirty young pilots arrived from England.
The commander, Lieutenant Colonel Kenneth Reid Van
der Spuy, was from South Africa, while the deputy
commander, Lieutenant Colonel Robin Grey, was English.
Almost half of the thirty pilots and observers were
from Canada. Fresh from flight training in England,
most had no more than twenty hours of flight time.
Far more experienced were twenty-seven Russian
aviators, veterans of the Russian Flying Corps, whose
bravery and skill came as a pleasant surprise.[12]

Four flying fields were maintained. The
headquarters was established at Archangel where two
permanent hangars were constructed. They featured
double walls insulated with sawdust, wooden floors,
wood-burning stoves, and such amenities as electric
lights and a telephone. Here was located the main
machine shop of the expedition, where 130 men were
kept busy assembling, repairing, and overhauling
aircraft. Nearby at Bakaritsa there was a long and
narrow (400-by-150-yard) field designed for winter
use. A seaplane station equipped with two wooden
hangars and a crane was also located here. Further
inland at Oberskaya, Flight A, equipped with DH-4s,
operated from a funnel-shaped clearing in the woods.
The fourth base was at Beresnik on the Dvina River,
from which Flight B flew Sopwith Strutters, RE-8s,
and Nieuport 17s. Only canvas hangers were available
at Oberskaya and Beresnik and in these, only minor
repairs were ordinarily performed.[13]

Keeping track of Bolshevik positions was the
first task of the novice flyers. To their discomfort
they soon discovered that the geography and climate
were of the most difficult nature imaginable. Few
natural landing places existed in the forests and
swamps of North Russia. Therefore, explained
Lieutenant Colonel Gray:

A forced landing when flying across
country is almost certain to mean a bad
crash, and at the best the loss of a
machine. Even if the crash should not be
very serious, extreme difficulty is
experienced in rendering assistance owing
to inaccessibility. Any machine forced to
land in swamp or forest can seldom, if at
all, be salved.

Even with a compass it is extremely
difficult to keep direction in these forests,
and going is very slow. Should both Pilot
and Observer be injured on crashing in the
forest the chances of their being saved are
nil. Even if only one of the occupants was
injured, the chances of rescuing him in time,
during the winter, are exceedingly small, as
the temperature at night frequently exceeds
60 degrees (Fahr.) of frost. Apart from this
the relief party would in all probability be
unable to find the machine.[14]

Engine failure was a depressingly frequent
occurrence. With the ever present possibility of
mechanical trouble in mind, the pilots were instructed
to keep either the railroad or the river in sight at
all times. By so doing it was hoped to facilitate
rescues and to avoid the possibility of pilots
becoming lost over the heavily forested terrain. The
least reliable of the aircraft were the DH-4s and the
RE-8s. In a typical incident a DH-4 returning from a
bombing raid crashed in a swamp thirty miles south of
Archangel when the engine "conked." The pilot and
observer, who were luckily unhurt, struggled through
five miles of forest and knee-deep slime until they
came to the railroad and safety. The first search
party sent to salvage the wreckage was unable to
locate the machine. On the second attempt the plane
was found with the aid of bearings provided from the
air. Despite clouds of mosquitoes, thirty laborers
then constructed a road of logs and, over a five-day
period, dragged the fuselage to the railroad. In the
end it was concluded that the plane was so badly
damaged as not to have been worth such an extensive
salvage effort.[15]
Six RE-8s which left Archangel for Beresnik also
developed problems. Only five planes arrived, because
the motor of the sixth jammed in the air causing the
propeller to break apart. Fortunately the pilot was
able to land in a frozen marsh and was brought out
the next day by woodcutters using a sleigh. Another
of the RE-8s was soon lost when it was struck by
machine-gun fire and crashed in trees in Bolshevik-
controlled territory. The two Canadian pilots,
believing they were too close to the enemy to burn
the wreckage, left their "bus" in the trees and
marched northward through deep snow. Suffering from
exhaustion and frostbitten feet, they reached the
Allied lines three days later. A few days afterward
two other Canadians experienced a close call when it
was discovered that a bullet had pierced their control

column without, for some reason, striking either
the pilot or observer. Not so fortunate were two
Russian flyers who were killed when their plane was
hit by machine-gun fire and crashed out of control
from an elevation of 1,000 feet. Due to the volume
and accuracy of Bolshevik ground fire, the Allied
aviators became a good deal more careful about flying
lower than was absolutely necessary.[16]

Overloading by the inexperienced ground crews
at Beresnik accounted for the disabling of another
RE-8. On the day of the Armistice a British pilot,
accompanied by observer Frank Shrive of Hamilton,
Ontario, attempted to take off with four twenty-pound
Cooper bombs under each wing, in addition to four
drums of machine-gun ammunition and a 200-pound bomb
attached to the undercarriage. The plane managed to
become airborne, but in the process struck a stump,
lost its left wheel, and suffered serious damage to
the wing stabilizer wires. Shrive was then ordered
to "drop those bloody bombs," but due to a jammed
cable only the four under the right wing released,
falling near the headquarters and causing "one hell
of a panic." The 200-pounder was disposed of over
the river (where the explosion lifted the crippled
plane some fifty feet and awoke the town of Beresnik).
Finally, the pilot managed to crash land on the right
wheel with four bombs hanging from their safety hooks.
Except for a badly smashed plane, the only serious
damage was sustained by the outhouse at headquarters
which required extensive remodeling. "Quite a day,"
noted Shrive in his diary, "and I have learned why the
R.[ussian] F.[lying] C.[orps] and now the R.[oyal]
A.[ir] F.[orce] are reputed to be prone to good
whiskey."[17]

The observer's taste for this potent British
beverage was no doubt stimulated by a narrow brush
with disaster experienced during his next flight in
an RE-8. Taking the place of a sick observer, Shrive
accompanied an English pilot who was instructed to
bomb a house with a blue roof located at a village
fifteen miles inside Bolshevik territory. Once the
target was reached it was discovered that all the
roofs were covered with snow and "we couldn't tell
one from another." As a compromise, the eight Cooper
bombs were dropped on several river barges that were
the nearest available target. Next the village was
showered with propaganda leaflets. However, some of
the paper leaflets jammed in the rudder control wires
so that the plane was able to turn in one direction
only. The solution was for Shrive to crawl on his
stomach to the tail, punch a hole through the fabric,
and remove the leaflets. "This I did," he recorded,

"but getting back to the cockpit was another matter,
as my feet threatened to go through the bottom canvas,
and to be honest I sure was scared." To prevent a
reoccurrence of this "harrowing experience," it was
decided in the future to insert propaganda leaflets
inside of cigarette packages containing one cigarette
each so as to avoid fouling the rudder control
wires.[18]

   With the arrival of winter the Allies' aviation
apparatus had progressed from a curiosity to a
valuable force for reconnaissance, for bombing
Bolshevik boats, guns, and villages, as well as
for directing artillery fire and distributing
propaganda. Ordinarily flying would have been
suspended during the months of intense cold so
as not to risk unnecessarily the planes and pilots.
Unfortunately for the Allies, the Bolsheviks had
no intention of sitting out the winter.

5

Some Unpleasant Surprises

For the first two months the North Russian campaign
was a modest success. Almost immediately General
Poole realized that he had no chance of reaching
Vologda or Kotlas before winter. Therefore, Poole
concentrated upon securing what he had already
occupied and upon recruiting an army of Russians that
was optimistically expected to reach 15,000 or 20,000.
Led by the French, Allied troops were able to
penetrate south 100 miles on the Vologda Railroad.
On the Dvina and its tributary the Vaga the British
and Americans also made impressive progress by
capturing the cities of Tulgas and Shenkursk. The
latter was regarded as the most important city of the
region except for Archangel. And in the third week
of October a company of Americans traveling by barge
easily occupied Pinega, a city of 3,000 inhabitants,
and several nearby villages.

Unlike the fighting in France, the front was not
continuous. The Allies only held strategic strong
points; great expanses of swamp, forest, and tundra
were left unoccupied. In developing what General
Finlayson called "a forward protective screen," it was
necessary to establish good lateral communications.
The British objective was to base the defense on a
line extending in the west from Onega to Plesetskaya
(on the railroad) to Shenkursk (on the Vaga) to
Puchega (on the Dvina). As it turned out, two of the
objectives were unattainable: the Allies were unable
to capture either Plesetskaya or Puchega. In his
memoirs, General Ironside graciously credited Poole
with having achieved much "with great dash and
vigour." Writing to the War Office on 8 November
1918, Ironside also praised Poole. "I think," he
stated, "that what has already been done by the
military command here is extraordinary as the material
they have had to deal with has been so extraordinarily

bad both from physique and training." Yet, as the
American John Cudahy noted in his memoir of the
campaign, ". . .before these forces had been halted,
already the Vaga Expedition had gone too far, thrust
out nearly one hundred miles from the Railway, and
fifty miles further south than the Dvina River party,
it presented inviting opportunity for enemy
encirclement."[1]

For the Allies and their new British commander
some unpleasant surprises were in store. One shock
was the realization that the Bolsheviks had no
intention of suspending the fighting. General
Finlayson, the highly regarded officer whom Ironside
appointed to command the Allied forces on the river,
expressed the generally held view when he wrote on
8 October, "It is believed that the Bolsheviks will
close down operations for the winter. I. . . cannot
imagine that in the present state of the weather and
the roads the enemy will attempt to move this side of
Kotlas." Yet the Bolsheviks, displaying superiority
in long-range artillery, unexpectedly renewed the
campaign on 19 October. Two weeks previously the
British naval flotilla on the Dvina, fearing the
imminent freezing of the river, had returned to
Archangel. The withdrawal, which left the Dvina
Force without heavy artillery support, was premature
by at least a month. Exploiting their advantage,
the Bolshevik flotilla of twenty boats supported by
1,700 infantry launched an artillery barrage which,
Ironside reported, "outclassed and outranged our
field battery. . . . Four eighteen-pound guns and
some Vickers machine guns had to be abandoned after
being rendered useless." The Bolshevik attack,
Finlayson recalled, "completely overpowered our
troops," forcing them to retreat ten miles from
Seltso to a new defensive line at Tulgas. The
disparity in artillery continued after the freezing
of the Dvina in early November as the Bolsheviks
unloaded their guns for winter use. "Thus," concluded
Ironside, "he was better in his information by 3 weeks
and caused us considerable annoyance and losses."[2]

The third month of the campaign also revealed
severe shortcomings in the training, leadership, and
morale of the Allied forces, especially on the river
front. Just a month after arriving at Archangel,
Ironside reported that he had received two major
impressions concerning the forces under his command:
"1. The poor quality of the Commanders sent out to
Russia [and] 2. The poor quality of the troops." Only
the best troops and commanders, he maintained, could
be expected to cope with the extended fronts and
isolated conditions. "The distances are enormous,"

Ironside pointed out. "Forces are completely isolated
when they have started and if the Column Commander
has not a stout heart things go wrong at once. The
responsibility upon one of these Column Commanders
is very much greater than on a Battalion Commander
in France and yet the level of such officers is
exceedingly low and a very large number of them have
not the slightest knowledge of military matters."[3]
     Illustrative of these deficiencies was the
sorry performance of a company of Royal Scots,
members of a famous regiment, when they, together
with a company of Russians and Poles, attacked Kuliga
village, between Tulgas and Seltso on 27 October.
Apparently a Bolshevik spy had alerted the defenders,
who launched a vigorous counterattack that cost
seventy-seven Allied casualties. Only the Poles and
eight Canadian and British artillery men performed
well in covering the Allied retreat. "These men,"
Finlayson reported, "behaved themselves as soldiers
should, were the last to withdraw and in consequence
came away unharmed, having made their presence very
severely felt by the enemy." But both the Russians
and the Royal Scots succumbed to panic. At the first
sight of the enemy the Russians bolted and, after
their officers were killed, two platoons of Royal
Scots likewise fled. When Finlayson questioned
several of the Scots as to why they had lost their
arms and equipment, "the answer generally received
was 'they prevented me from running fast enough'
and the speakers in some cases were not ashamed of
themselves at all. In other cases the men said 'this
is not the kind of work for 'B' category men to have
to do and we never expected it.'"
     In Finlayson's opinion much of the explanation for
the poor showing was that none of the men had been a
soldier before the war and only 10 percent had seen
service in France. "Add to that," he noted, "the fact
that all these men were told by the doctors in England
that they were not fit for fighting, or marching, but
that they would have a 'cushy holiday' in Russia, then
one can see the difficulties which present themselves
with every move." Only a thorough reorganization and
reinforcement could remedy the troops' "faint
heartedness." In the opinion of Ironside the Royal
Scots were "certainly not fit to carry out active
operations either in France or Russia. They might
have carried out Garrison duties but that is all."
From a purely military standpoint the setback was not
of great significance, but the psychological effect
was devastating. "Such a minor disaster," Ironside
wrote, ". . . cannot but have the worst effect upon
the people of this country who look to us as warlike

people who have come to assist them." As a result
of the fiasco at Kuliga, concluded Finlayson, "British
prestige is suffering very greatly, not only in the
eyes of our friends the Poles, the Americans and the
few Russians who help us, but we are descending
without a doubt in the eyes of even the Bolsheviks."[4]

According to a memorandum possessed by Colonel
George Stewart, the commander of the 339th Infantry,
the Royal Scots--about two weeks after their
disgraceful performance at Kuliga--further besmirched
their already tarnished reputation. Stewart's
memorandum was provided by First Lieutenant Charles
E. Lewis and purported to be "a true extract" from
a confidential report filed by General Finlayson in
which he described an attack on 14 November by 140
Bolsheviks upon a village that constituted the outer
defenses on the west bank of the Dvina.

> This village was held by 30 Royal Scots
> under Lt. Dalziel. The result of this attack
> for us was not glorious for Lt. Dalziel
> appears to have been the only man who showed
> any resistance. He was shot through the neck
> in the first few minutes and thereupon the
> whole of the rest of the men took to flight,
> even passing Lieut. Dalziel as he lay upon
> the ground wounded and not even offering to
> help carry him away.
> A woman inhabitant of the village
> reports that Lt. Dalziel could not stand
> up as the Bolsheviks approached, but raised
> himself on his elbow and attempted to draw
> his revolver, whereupon two Bolsheviks
> stepped up to him and clubbed him on the head
> with their rifle butts, killing him outright.
> His body was recovered later, and its
> appearance helps to bear out this statement.

Just how Lewis acquired the Finlayson report is not
clear. But although the original has apparently
not survived, Stewart's memorandum appears to be
authentic; its writing is stylistically similar
to that of Finlayson's and the unsavory incident
described is not dissimilar from the conduct of the
Royal Scots at Kuliga. The accumulation of such
troubles may well have contributed to the exhaustion
of General Finlayson, who in December was ordered by
his doctors to return to England. For Ironside the
departure of Finlayson was "a severe blow," as there
was no experienced replacement available to take his
place.[5]

The 1,650-man French Colonial Infantry received far more favorable reviews during its first two months in the field. But by October the French were physically tired and demoralized by rumors of an armistice on the western front. Moreover, the French commander, in Ironside's opinion, "proved himself weak and useless." On two separate occasions the French troops on the railroad refused to obey orders to advance toward Plesetskaya. As a result, reported Ironside, "I had personally to go and interview both officers and men accompanied by the French Military Attaché." The battalion, he found, was "in a thoroughly disaffected state. The men, encouraged by some of the younger officers, have openly stated that, if there is an armistice in France, they do not intend to fight and this attitude was acquiesced in by the Battalion Commander, hence the increase in ill-discipline in the Battalion." Despite the efforts of Ironside and French ambassador Noulens to restore order, the French soon degenerated into what Finlayson termed "a sullen band of strikers and shirkers, who increase the difficulties of the commander enormously."[6]

Worst of all the Allied troops, in the opinion of the British generals, were the Americans. Of the 339th Infantry, Ironside observed: "I have seen many American Regiments in France and had them under my command but I have never seen anything quite so bad as this Regiment which consists of a very large proportion of foreigners--Poles, Russians and Jews." Many of the soldiers from Detroit, complained Finlayson, "cannot even speak English." In Ironside's opinion "this was the very worst class of material to send out to Russia," because the Russian-speaking soldiers were easily influenced by Bolshevik ideas and propaganda which they disseminated to their fellows. Ironside conceded that the Americans, unlike the disaffected French, would obey orders, but his estimate of the military value of the 339th Infantry was devastating: "The Regiment had received absolutely no training and the officers were, one and all, of the lowest value imaginable." Without exception the officers were "quite incapable of commanding any force of any size. They are inexperienced to a degree that I have never seen before in American troops in France." On one occasion, stated Ironside, the American troops "behaved exceedingly badly and I do not think that this Regiment is fit to carry out active operations." General Finlayson concurred in Ironside's assessment, noting that while a few members of the 339th Infantry were "truly American and stouthearted," the majority

were "not soldiers, never will be and show a very poor
morale."[7]   The only American contingent to escape the
wrath of the British generals was the 310th Engineers
whose skill in repairing bridges and constructing
defenses won consistent praise.

Much of the blame for the apparent ineptness
of the 339th Infantry was placed at the door of its
commander, Colonel George E. Stewart.   According to
Ironside, Colonel Stewart was "not a man of much
energy. . . . His Regiment has been divided up with
various columns and he himself has taken no command
in military operations. I do not think he would have
been capable of undertaking any operations."   This
critical assessment was written not long after
Ironside had had a "disappointing" interview with
Stewart in the colonel's Archangel office.   To
Stewart's surprise, Ironside asked him to take over
command of the railroad front.   After thinking the
offer over for a few minutes, Stewart declined on the
ground he would be exceeding his instructions if he
were to leave Archangel.   And even though Ironside
"pressed him hard" he would not change his mind.
Soon Ironside recorded that Stewart was having a
"particularly hard time" in controlling serious
misconduct on the part of his officers. "We have
had numerous cases amongst the American Officers
from living with women to selling the men's rations
and embezzlement of funds.   There have been cases of
cowardice also." Furthermore, complained Ironside,
Stewart was either unwilling or unable to make the
American soldiers assigned as warehouse sentries
"understand that they were there to stop and not to
aid the wholesale thieving that was going on.   The
American sentries thieved as much as anybody else
and we have definitely caught an American sergeant
deliberately taking away flour in a motor." General
Wilds P. Richardson, who succeeded Stewart as American
commander in April 1919, also criticized the colonel
for failing to prevent pilfering and trafficking in
supplies by American troops.   "It is this fact,"
noted Richardson, "which makes it impossible for
me to recommend Colonel Stewart for an award for
meritorious service in this Northern Russian
Campaign."[8]

Only General Poole seems to have been more
unpopular than Colonel Stewart.   Practically no one,
either at the time or afterward, had much praise for
him.   Soldiers who served under Stewart criticized
him for remaining in Archangel with the "steam heat"
troops while they served in the field under severe
conditions.   He was accused of having weakly abandoned
his command to the British, and criticized for failing

to offer a coherent explanation as to why the
expedition was fighting in Russia at all. One soldier
bluntly concluded: "He was not a great success as a
commanding officer. He fell down weakly under his
great responsibility." An even blunter judgment came
from another soldier who recalled Stewart as "our
very weak half-assed commander."[9] Nevertheless, his
qualifications appeared to well suit Stewart for his
difficult assignment. At the age of nineteen, Stewart
had immigrated to the United States from his native
Australia. Entering the army as a private in 1896, he
rose rapidly to the rank of second lieutenant in 1899.
That same year he distinguished himself during the
Philippine Insurrection by winning the Congressional
Medal of Honor. "While crossing a river in the face
of the enemy," read his citation, "this officer
plunged in and at immediate risk of his own life
saved from drowning an enlisted man of his regiment."
Promotions to first lieutenant and captain soon
followed. From 1908 to 1910 Stewart was commander
of a post in Alaska and he found that experience
"was invaluable to me when I went to about the same
latitude in Russia during the war." Once America
entered World War I, experienced military men were
in short supply and Stewart quickly advanced to
major in 1917 and to colonel a year later. He was
forty-six years old when he arrived at Archangel.[10]

     Almost immediately Stewart found himself in an
untenable position. Everything that went wrong was
blamed on him. He was criticized by the British for
the failure of the railway column to capture Vologda.
And the American troops blamed him for the British
food ration and delays in the sending of winter
equipment. No doubt Stewart was confused as to what
his role should be. A few weeks after arriving at
Archangel, Stewart was told by the War Department that
"for tactical purposes and for administrative matters
involving the entire command" he was to follow the
orders of the British commander. Only "matters of
internal administration" remained under Stewart's
jurisdiction. Most of his time was, therefore, spent
in Archangel attempting with a small staff to cope
with bureaucratic details. Ironside urged Stewart to
leave his headquarters and make frequent trips to the
field "so that his men could see that he was still in
command." But to visit his troops invariably placed
Stewart in a humiliating position, since his men were
serving under the British flag and under British
officers. To all observers it must have been obvious
that Stewart was not in command and was basically
powerless. On one occasion Ironside asked Stewart
to send him the names of soldiers who were performing

good work so that he might award them ribbons and medals. "'I replied,' recorded the frustrated Colonel, 'I would give millions to have the power to do that.'"[11]

In his occasional visits to the troops Stewart, instead of inspiring confidence, invariably created a bad impression. During a short trip to the railroad front in October, for example, the colonel appeared to be preoccupied and hurriedly left for Archangel without taking the time to attend a funeral service for three Americans. As First Lieutenant P. I. Bukowski pointed out, the troops were resentful since "they expected their Colonel to be present at the ceremony of burial of his first three men killed in action, which he could have done by remaining five minutes additional to what he had already remained." At Shenkursk, two months later, Stewart dropped his mitten on a porch and made himself appear foolish by insinuating that someone had stolen it. Neither was Stewart, nor anyone else for that matter, able to provide a convincing rationale for fighting a war against the Bolsheviks. Addressing troops on the Dvina front, Stewart remarked that his work at Archangel was just as difficult as theirs, if not more so. The soldiers, reported their commander, "were very disappointed by the talk he made to them as it did not explain what they were here for."[12]

Possibly Stewart erred by rejecting Ironside's offer to become commander of the railroad front. However, acceptance of the position would not have altered the fact that he was essentially a high-level clerk who ranked beneath Ironside and Ambassador Francis in the Archangel power structure. The departure of the ill ambassador on the Olympia in early November left Stewart as the highest ranking American at Archangel, but the colonel still had little voice in determining the disposition of the American troops. Perhaps a more politically minded leader might have been more successful in establishing rapport with the infantrymen and in inspiring respect for his office. But fundamentally the troops were complaining not so much about Stewart's policies, but about being ordered to fight in Russia after the war had ended in Europe. Essentially his position was an impossible one and it is hardly surprising that the embattled colonel developed a painful case of stomach ulcers besides suffering an attack of acute eczema. According to General Richardson, much of the criticism of the American commander was attributable to "Colonel Stewart's temperament and to a certain lack of diplomatic finesse." Also, as Richardson pointed out, Stewart was sent to Russia "without an experienced and

competent staff" and as a result Stewart was overly
burdened with administrative details. In his own
defense, Stewart maintained that his critics "only
knew of what occurred in their own little area."
Therefore, they had little appreciation of the
overall situation and simplistically blamed Stewart
for their troubles.[13]

A further disappointment for Ironside was the
unspectacular pace of recruiting among the Russian
population. A prime assumption of British policy
had been that the Allied landing would produce a
"revulsion of feeling" that would lead to the
appearance of a substantial anti-Bolshevik army.
Under Poole the main recruiting effort was directed
toward organizing a Slavo-British Legion. But only
about three thousand "motley" volunteers came forth
and of these only five hundred were fit for service.
To the Americans the apathetic response of the
Russians was incomprehensible considering the stakes
involved. As expressed by First Lieutenant William
F. Higgins: "These people are fighting for their own
homes, families and their lives and really everything
they have, and I never saw a bigger bunch of cowards.
They won't turn over a hand to help themselves. They
expect us to do it all." "The Russian is totally
averse to any voluntary action on his own part,"
Ironside observed. "Order him, and he will do what
you order him to do, but of initiative he has none."
According to an American observer, the members of the
Slavo-British Legion were "utterly unreliable--they
are in it only for the food they get--rationnaires
as the French say."[14]

Far more emphasis was placed upon developing a
Russian National Army through a general mobilization
that began in earnest during the month of October.
Eventually almost 18,000 troops of questionable
ability were gathered, but initial progress was
unimpressive. The Chaikovsky government, which
had been briefly deposed by Chaplin's military coup,
proved extremely cautious about creating an army
which might be used against it. As of 1 October only
1,500 troops had joined the new army and they were
characterized by Ironside as "mostly old soldiers and
returned prisoners of war, unorganized and distinctly
mutinous." Finding qualified Russian officers to lead
these troops proved a serious problem for Ironside.
Neither Governor General Boris Douroff nor Chief of
Staff T. Samarin "were possessed of any outstanding
qualities." Douroff had gained his position, Ironside
claimed, by "ingratiating" himself with President
Chaikovsky, but he was "weak and without energy."
Samarin, in Ironside's opinion, was even worse. "He

is a man of no military value and knows it. None
of the old regime officers will serve under him,"
Ironside reported. "He it was who signed the order
abolishing saluting in the Russian Army [under the
Provisional Government of Alexander Kerensky]. He
was absolutely unsuited for his position; I might
even call him stupid."[15]

The dispute between Ironside and the generals
appointed by Chaikovsky came to a head on 31 October
when the Archangel Regiment of the Russian National
Army refused an order by Samarin to parade. The men
shouted "We will not salute," "Increase the bread
ration," and "Abolish the order concerning saluting."
Samarin then interviewed the soldiers "allowing them
to crowd round with cigarettes in their mouths while
explaining their grievances." Samarin stated that no
attention need be paid the requirement that soldiers
must salute their officers. Ironside was especially
outraged to learn that "General Samarin actually used
the word Tovarish or comrade to one soldier, and said
that he was glad to shake hands with a true Russian
who would not be ordered about by foreign officers.
I at once saw the President and informed him that
if Douroff and Samarin did not resign by 12 noon
that day I should at once try them by Court Martial
for inciting mutiny and discontent. After a stormy
interview I gained my point." The next day
(2 November) the elderly president reluctantly
removed both men from office. Douroff then went into
exile in England, while Samarin enlisted as a private
in the French foreign legion. His immediate superior
was Corporal Leonid I. Strakhovsky, who later
distinguished himself as the author of the standard
scholarly study of the Archangel intervention.
Actually Samarin was only a private for a few months
before being made a captain and a company commander.[16]

The undisciplined condition of the Russian troops
at Archangel continued for the next few weeks despite
Ironside's efforts to force the men to work under the
direction of British officers. But in Ironside's
opinion the British training staff was itself
deficient. The officers selected as instructors,
complained Ironside, appeared to have been culled from
"the scum of the officers of England," and the general
found it necessary to return several "useless"
alcoholic officers to England. "I quite realise the
difficulties of selecting officers for a 'side show'
like this," Ironside stated, "but a drunken officer is
the worst kind of man to send to this country where he
may be sent to an isolated post under no supervision."
Likewise, President Chaikovsky was not much help in
establishing military discipline. Despite the mutiny,

the elderly president continued to believe that a
democratic army could be created on the Kerensky
model. And he immersed himself in such bureaucratic
minutiae as personally writing a decree abolishing
the office of assistant governor-general for civil
affairs, and in issuing "Regulations pertaining to
the proper procedure during the meetings of the
Provisional Government," "Estimates of expenditures
for salaries of the Regional State Bank," and
"Changes to be effected in the wording of some
articles of the Postal-Telegraph statutes. . . ."[17]

A slight improvement in discipline occurred
following the arrival from Paris on 17 November of
General Vladimir V. Marushevsky. He had previously
commanded Russian troops on the western front, but
Marushevsky was a strange choice as a disciplinarian
because of his diminutive stature. In contrast to
the six-foot-four Ironside, he stood only about five
feet tall and the soldiers said of him: "Whether he
sits or stands it is all the same." Upon his arrival
Ironside informed Marushevsky that "we must enforce
discipline at once and deal with any trouble with a
severe hand, and that I was prepared to support him."
After three weeks of drilling the two generals agreed
that the time had come "to put the matter of
discipline to the test." Thus, on the afternoon
of 11 December, Ironside ordered a parade of the
1,730-man Archangel Regiment prior to its being sent
to the railroad front. Instead of turning out as
ordered the men mutinied and locked themselves in the
Alexander Nevsky barracks. "The situation was easily
dealt with," Ironside recounted, "by firing a couple
of rounds from a Stokes Mortar into the Barracks.
The men came out quickly and fell in, delivering up
thirteen men voluntarily as the leaders of the mutiny,
and these were executed at once."[18] Although the
regiment departed for the front only three hours
behind schedule the incident was hardly reassuring.
Nor was the execution of thirteen men, without even
the pretense of a trial, a flattering commentary on
the democratic principles of the North Russian
government.

Morale among the American and western European
troops was certainly far better than among the
Russians. In fact, the signing of the Armistice
on 11 November 1918 produced a general mood of
elation as the troops believed that the end of the
war in France meant that their war was about to end
as well. "Wild reports of immediate demobilisation
at home, and the impossibility of giving a definite
policy aggravated matters," noted Ironside. Until
the Armistice the campaign had been justified as

essential to contain German ambitions in Russia.
After the Armistice the purpose of the mission was
decidedly ambivalent. When the Y.M.C.A. worker Ralph
Albertson toured the fronts in December he found that
"Everywhere, on every occasion, I was asked
persistently and importunately, 'What are we here
for?' 'The Armistice is signed, why are we fighting?'
'What have we against the Bolsheviki?' The American
and Canadian troops were particularly outspoken in
their resentment at being at war in a futile fight
against nobody and for nothing in particular when the
rest of the world had stopped fighting." Ironside
reported that he was forced to spend much of his time
combatting talk among British officers "the tenour of
which has been 'We've done our bit, why stay and fight
for these damned Russians, who have always let us
down.'"[19]

If the British troops were inclined to blame the
Russians for their difficulties, the dispirited
Americans universally blamed the British. Antagonism
between the two "allies" dated from the first day of
the campaign. General Poole inaugurated a policy of
elevating British officers to temporary ranks higher
than those of the other Allied officers. From the
British point of view it was only sensible for their
officers to outrank those of their allies so as to
insure a logical chain of command. In a conversation
with Colonel Stewart, Ironside defended the practice
on the ground that only the British had provided
"troops of all arms and a complete service of
administration." In practice, lower-ranking British
officers were frequently less than tactful. In the
words of Ralph Albertson: "They set their own petty
officers upon the Americans in a manner that was most
irritating to American national self-esteem and
bitterly resented." Albertson also recalled hearing
English soldiers singing an insulting version of the
popular song "Over There," which began with "The
Yanks are running, the Yanks are running everywhere,"
and concluded, "And they didn't do a damn thing about
it over there." General Wilds P. Richardson also
found an overbearing spirit of superiority on the part
of the British command. British policy, Richardson
reported, "has not been one, in any sense, of
cooperation with their Allies, but merely of employing
such forces as were obtainable from the other Allies,
subordinated in every sense to British dictation."
Soon after his arrival in April 1919, said Richardson,
he discovered that "I would fulfill the expectations
concerning myself, provided that I should see that
the troops under me obeyed the orders issued by
the British command, and that my officers and men

conducted themselves with due and proper respect to
officers in the British service."[20]
Among American infantrymen virulent Anglophobia
was widespread. One soldier, whose letter was
discovered by military censors, unwisely wrote,

> We are under British control. Mind you
> the English own us; they can do with us as
> they please. Good God you can't beleave how
> those English are hated round here. They
> have Officers that out rank our officers. If
> one of our Officers is promoted as high as
> theirs, they promote one higher again. And
> just think we must do as they say and the God
> damn fools are of more harm than good. They
> can't fight.
>   Would you beleave it? We haven't enough
> men or supplies to fight with. The Bolos
> [slang for Bolsheviks] have better Artillery
> than we have and they can use it also. Of
> course its English doings. But think of the
> disgrace to the Americans who are pushed in
> to this dead fire by those English, and must
> back water, which an American hates to do.
> It's hell I'm telling you.

Another soldier was detected writing "contemptuous
and disrespectful words" against the president of the
United States for expressing the view that British
diplomats "pulled the wool" over Woodrow Wilson's
eyes and for saying that Wilson had permitted the
339th Infantry to be used as "mere toys in the hands
of Englishmen." Lieutenant Henry Katz, who had
written "censored, O.K." on the envelope containing
the critical epistle, was directed to explain "why
it was that he made such endorsement upon a letter
containing such criticisms of the President, of the
conduct and policy of the Government and of our
British allies."[21]
General Ironside was not held personally
responsible by the Americans for their difficulties.
A consummate politician, Ironside established a
universal reputation for fairness. According to
John Cudahy, Ironside conducted the campaign with
"inspiring leadership, with unfailing heartsome
courage; and he won the sympathy of all by his rare
tact and understanding." General Richardson, who
was very unimpressed with the overall quality of the
British officers, was another enthusiastic admirer.
In his final report on operations, Richardson wrote:
"High credit, in my judgment and the judgment of
all with whom I have spoken, is due to the Allied

Commander-in-Chief, Major General Ironside, for his resolute spirit and inspiring example of soldierly qualities, coupled with rare good judgment in the exercise of command over these diverse and restless elements."[22]

Yet, Ironside had great difficulty in impressing on many of his arrogant and supercilious officers the wisdom of following his own example of tactful leadership. In the tradition of General Poole, the British officer corps often displayed a spirit of contemptuous superiority such as was customary in dealing with native troops of the British Empire. As one soldier summed up the American dilemma: "So there we were--British food, British tobacco, Russian guns and under the command of the British." Declining hours of daylight, bitterly cold weather, the closing of Archangel by ice, and the realization that there was no end in sight to the campaign further added to the general feeling of melancholia. At least the dispirited American troops in the field were furnished the same liquor allowance as the British. "The value of the rum ration was more proved than ever," concluded Ironside, "and I wish I could have had some of the placid prohibitionists on sentry go for an hour in 74 degrees of frost, and they would have changed their opinions as to whether it should be issued or not."[23]

6

The Start of Winter Fighting

Demonstrating a familiarity with the terrain and
ignoring the arctic winter, the Bolsheviks gradually
took the offensive against the overextended Allied
forces. At 7:45 a.m. on 11 November, the very day
the war ended on the western front, the Bolsheviks
launched a surprise attack against the American
defenses at Tulgas on the west bank of the Dvina.
According to accounts obtained afterwards from
prisoners, the 600 attackers left Seltso on
9 November marching through woods and swamps
and camping without fires. Attacking across an
undefended marsh, the Bolsheviks came very close
to capturing the town. As recounted by Ironside,
the day was saved "by the exceedingly gallant
behavior of the drivers of a Canadian battery."
Reversing their guns, they opened fire at point-blank
range "and annihilated a strong enemy force which had
got round the rear of our forces and threatened them
with capture." The next day five enemy gunboats,
positioned just out of the range of the Canadian
artillery, took advantage of thawing conditions to
unleash a devastating barrage. Much of the damage
was inflicted by a barge armed with two six-inch guns.
As described by one diarist:

> At 8 a.m. a shell hit the hay stack
> a few feet from us, at 10 a.m. they were
> dropping all around. . . at 11 a.m. one hit
> the base of the blockhouse covering our
> Vickers [machine gun] with sand. At 11:30
> one hit the roof--3 killed and 5 wounded, a
> piece of shell went in my hand and shoulder,
> we crawled out and they opened fire, a bullet
> went through my overcoat, crawled to first
> house, there's a horrible sight inside, the
> whole family outside of a little girl, lay

killed. [Private Charles] Bell was lying
there seriously wounded, helped dress wounds,
a shell hit the building as we lay huddled
together, finally darkness came and with
that our relief, feel all broken up inside.[1]

For the next two days the sleepless Americans
were subjected to constant artillery fire. Yet the
Bolsheviks were apparently too weakened to attempt
further ground assaults. Furthermore, British
airplanes from Beresnik aided the American defenders
by bombing and machine gunning the Bolshevik flotilla.
Not so helpful, however, was a strangely timed
telegram sent to Captain Robert Boyd by the British
quartermaster from the opposite side of the Dvina.
Despite the constant shelling, Boyd was instructed
immediately to account for thirty-six scarves for
which proper receipts had not been issued. Finally,
on 14 November as snow began falling, the Bolshevik
shelling slackened and the exhausted Americans
launched a counterattack that regained their original
position. To improve the defenses of Tulgas the
Allies proceeded to burn the small village of Upper
Tulgas after giving the despairing inhabitants three
hours to remove their possessions.[2]

Meanwhile the Vaga column experienced increased
pressure. Lieutenant Glen Weeks, who was stationed
at the most advanced American outpost of Ust Padenga
(located eighteen miles from Shenkursk), recorded in
his diary numerous instances of increased Bolshevik
activity. On 13 November a four-man patrol fell
into a trap from which only one escaped. The three
victims were "mutilated sadly." Four days later "we
caught two spies trying to find out our position,
outpost strength, etc. Lieutenant [Francis W.] Cuff
[of Rio, Wisconsin], Lieutenant [J.D.] Winslow [of
the Canadian Field Artillery], and myself took one
of them out in the woods and shot him." The next
day in honor of the first sunny day in three weeks,
the officers "went out and buried [the] spy." On
29 November an American patrol of sixty men, seeking
to discover the exact location of the Bolsheviks,
ran into a strongly defended position in a forest
clearing. An enemy force estimated at 400 men
tried to surround the Americans who hastily
retreated, being "severely handled in the process."
Fifteen Americans died including Lieutenant Cuff,
who "was killed after he was almost out of the
enemy territory." Several stories were distributed
concerning Cuff's death. According to the original
version, the enemy severed the dead lieutenant's
arms and legs with axes. A more dramatic, if less

believable, account surfaced during Cuff's funeral at
Shenkursk when an American captain delivered a short
speech. According to medical corpsman G. L. Anderson,
the captain stated that the Bolsheviks had emasculated
the American officer, whereupon Cuff had killed
himself with his own pistol. "That is the kind
of enemy you are fighting," he warned.[3]

The circulation of dubious atrocity stories was
a tactic used frequently by both sides to inspire
hatred of the opposition. The Bolsheviks were
accused of such bloodcurdling crimes as castrating
the wounded while they were still alive, ripping open
their abdomens, and cutting off their fingers, noses,
and ears. As one apprehensive British pilot noted in
his diary, "I should hate to have my tummy ripped
open in cold blood and my appendages removed. Ugh!"
And during a Bolshevik attack near Pinega an American
was observed throwing away his ring and exclaiming,
"They won't cut my finger off." Colonel Dilaktorsky,
a picturesque Cossack leader at Shenkursk, was
reported to have been shot by the Bolsheviks, his
body dismembered, and the various pieces thrown into
the firebox of a tugboat. Ironside, in his memoirs,
repeated this story, but with the more dramatic
addition that the colonel was supposedly thrown
into the firebox in one piece and while still living.
Not surprisingly the Bolsheviks also disseminated
horrifying atrocity stories involving the Allies. A
British aviator described a scene in which a Bolshevik
prisoner threw himself on the ground, clasped the
officer by the legs, and poured out a torrent of
pleading words in his native tongue, none of which
the officer could understand. Afterward the officer
learned that "the prisoner had been told by his
superiors that all men captured by the British were
automatically castrated, and he had rushed up to the
first British officer to explain that, if it were all
the same to me, he would much rather be left intact."[4]

Not all the atrocity stories were fabrications.
Diaries and memoirs of Allied participants, which are
far more numerous than the sanitized Soviet versions
of the conflict, contain numerous accounts of
brutality toward Bolshevik prisoners. According
to Ralph Albertson, the Allied officers routinely
instructed their men "to take no prisoners, to kill
them even if they came in unarmed, and I have been
told by the men themselves of many cases when this
was done." The prisoners who were taken, said
Albertson, were invariably robbed by their captors.
Corporal John Toornman, stationed at Pinega, recalled
that both sides in that district habitually shot
prisoners. He told also of being detailed to shoot

a White Russian officer who was compelled to dig his
own grave, and of disciplining an American soldier for
molesting a fifteen-year-old girl.   Twice Toornman was
sent by English intelligence officers in the middle
of the night to arrest suspected spies.   According to
his account,

> We would go with a couple of sleighs,
> mostly at night, surround the house so no
> one could get away, as there were no locks
> on the doors.   Someone would then go inside
> and get a light and get the family out of
> bed.   By this time all of us would be inside
> in order to get out of the cold.   Grandma,
> mother and the children were all crying by
> this time.   The husband was told to get
> dressed.   His wife gave him a couple of
> coins and we took him along.   A few days
> later a fellow whom I knew from Kalamazoo
> told me that they had taken the husband to
> the river, then stuck him with bayonets
> until he had backed into a hole in the ice.
> This was the place where everybody came to
> get water every day.   The man who was killed
> had been suspected of being a Bolo.

Soviet accounts of the Archangel intervention also
emphasized brutal treatment of prisoners, especially
at the White Russian prison camp on Mudyug Island.
On the other hand, ten American prisoners who were
eventually repatriated through Finland told of being
beaten, robbed, cursed, spat upon, starved, and
propagandized.   Once they reached Moscow, however,
their treatment abruptly improved and they were
permitted to tour the city virtually as tourists
prior to their release.[5]
   Once the conflict was over and passions had
cooled somewhat, several American participants were
willing to concede that the Bolsheviks had actually
been no more brutal than the Allies.   Ralph Albertson
told of hearing detailed stories, supposedly provided
by Allied spies, of Bolshevik murders, rapes, and
tortures.   Later he found that the accusations were
mostly groundless, and he could find no evidence the
Bolsheviks shot prisoners as did the Allies.   Even
the historians of the 339th Infantry conceded that
tales of Bolshevik atrocities were exaggerated by
90 percent.[6]   Reflecting the cruel conditions of the
North Russian civil war, both sides generally offered
no quarter to the opposition.   Despite the claims of
their respective propagandists, neither side had a
monopoly on virtue or on brutality.

During the month of December, Bolshevik probing
became more and more persistent and, in response,
Ironside ordered increased Allied patrol activity to
discover the enemy's strength. Learning that 200
Bolsheviks had occupied Kodema, located twenty miles
east of Shenkursk, Colonel C. Graham, the British
commander at Shenkursk, ordered a similar sized force
of Americans and Cossacks to recapture the place.
Weeks, who participated in the operation, recorded
that the column made its approach march at night
in a snowstorm. Arriving at Kodema at 5:45 a.m.
on 7 December, the troops prepared to attack but
abandoned the plan when "the pom pom [a small
one-pound cannon] would not work." Lieutenant
Henry Katz, who was assigned as regimental medical
officer, observed that the machine guns froze also
and therefore "we retired without firing a shot."
A week later Katz was present as a second American
attack on Kodema miscarried. Due to "some mistake in
orders" the frostbitten Americans failed to advance
in support of 100 attacking Cossacks. "It was very
cold and trip very hard on the men," he noted. A
completely different interpretation was recorded by
Ironside. In his view the attacks "failed owing to
the quality of the U.S. troops and the behaviour of
one of their officers, and gave the enemy an idea of
the value of our troops opposed to them."[7]
Then a few weeks later the 280-man Caucasian
Cossack Regiment, despite two months of training,
also failed in an attack upon Kodema. The operation
was preceded by a fierce demonstration in which the
Cossacks pledged eternal loyalty to their colonel
and promised to wreak dire destruction upon the foe.
Nevertheless, as recorded by Colonel Graham, "the
enemy were noticed to be in greater numbers than had
been expected, and in addition to the committing of
several tactical mistakes the Cossack cavalry got out
of hand and could not be rallied." Graham found it
necessary to send Weeks and his troops from Shenkursk
to gather stragglers and re-establish order.
Believing that their colonel had perished, the
returning Cossacks proceeded to loot the possessions
of their leader, only to discover a few days later
that the colonel was very much alive after all.
"For days thereafter," it was noted, "the garrison
resounded to the cracking of the Colonel's knout,
and this time the wailing and shedding of tears was
undoubtedly more real than any that had been shed
previously to that time." In Ironside's opinion
the disastrous performance of the Cossacks further
demonstrated to the Bolsheviks "the lack of value
of our troops."[8]

The setbacks suffered by both sides--at Tulgas
by the Bolsheviks and at Kodema by the Allies--
illustrated one of the major characteristics of
winter fighting in North Russia: the advantage
enjoyed by the defense. It was to a great extent
a war fought to defend the housing required to
protect the troops from the elements. As Ironside
pointed out,

> If your accommodation was destroyed,
> even to the extent of breaking your windows,
> you had to evacuate your position. Prolonged
> operations in the open were an impossibility.
> The defence had thus an enormous advantage.
> I found that many of the defences put up
> were false in principle, and I had to
> remodel the whole of them in consequence.
> They did not assure the accommodation. If
> the enemy could get up his guns and shell
> the accommodation he had you out in the end
> by sheer physical exhaustion from the cold.
> They had, therefore, to be designed to
> protect this accommodation efficiently, and
> the principle in the end became somewhat
> similar to the forts d'arret on mountain
> frontiers. If you blocked a road the enemy
> could not get his guns up, as it was too long
> and tedious to cut and make roads through
> the forest.

Moreover, the cold and snow, combined with the reduced
light and heavily forested terrain, had an insidious
effect upon the men's already frayed nerves. "Sentry
and patrol work in the forest was found a very nervy
business at first," observed Ironside. "Peering long
into a forest is dangerous to those who have not stout
hearts. I have interrogated many sentries on this
subject and always found the same state of mind. Of
course, no single sentries should be allowed under
any circumstances."[9]
Under arctic conditions even minor injuries
frequently proved fatal as the injured soldier was
likely to freeze to death before he could be rescued.
Ironside received a vivid illustration of the dangers
of winter fighting when he visited an American
blockhouse near Seletskoe at dusk on a frigid December
afternoon. A sentry suddenly challenged a Bolshevik
patrol, and the troops, from the security of the warm
blockhouse, responded with mortar and machine-gun
fire. After five minutes of silence, Ironside and an
American captain decided to investigate and observed
a chilling sight:

Some hundred yards beyond the wire we
came across six bodies lying in the snow.
They were dressed in long white smocks and
were on short skis, which were bound with
rough skins to keep them from slipping.
All were quite dead and frozen stiff in the
intense cold. Two had been wounded in the
legs and had died of exhaustion and loss of
blood. They must have died within a few
minutes of being hit.

The incident once again demonstrated to the British
commander the advantage of a strong defense under
arctic conditions.[10]

A good defense was needed all the more because
the arrival of snow and frigid temperatures severely
restricted the ability of the primitive R.A.F.
airplanes to lend assistance. Beginning in October
flying was hampered by shorter days, periodic snow
storms, and low temperatures. In November the lowest
temperature recorded was -10° Fahrenheit. December
was relatively mild with a low of only -5°; however,
in January the low temperature reached -40° and in
February, -53°. To cope with such extremes, the
flyers were issued silk gloves, socks, and underwear.
Over this was worn regular wool winter clothing and
the "Sidcot suit," consisting of electrically heated
gloves, insoles, and waistcoat. Once in the airplane,
the electrically heated units were plugged in with
the power being supplied by a wing-mounted generator.
Notwithstanding these precautions, frostbite was a
common occurrence.

For the mechanics, the hardships created by such
conditions were enormous. The extreme cold made it
almost impossible to handle tools or metal. "Minor
adjustments to machines or engines," noted Lieutenant
Colonel Robin Grey, "which under ordinary conditions
would take but a few minutes, frequently occupied
a party of men a very considerable time." Great
amounts of energy were also expended shoveling snow
from hangar roofs and thawing the frozen curtains and
ropes of the canvas hangars. As Frank Shrive noted
in his diary: "Our hangars are no protection from
the cold, as they are just canvas tents, and except
for keeping the snow from the machines do little
other good. The mechanics have a ruddy cold job and
we all think they are a fine bunch of fellows. The
lads who take care of the machine guns do have a
small shack with a stove in it; it would be almost
impossible to load the drums out in the open as bare
hands would stick to the metal, and you just can't
load drums with heavy gloves on."[11]

Engines had to be insulated with thick-padded engine covers augmented by six or more flameless lamps. Even so there was constant trouble with radiators cracking while empty, despite maximum efforts to keep them warm. Numerous instances were recorded of flying wires snapping on landing due to the extreme cold. Grey's account of an attempt to fly a DH-4, which was equipped with a water-cooled R.A.F. 3A engine, provides a graphic example of the mechanical difficulties encountered:

From December 6th, 1918, a D.H. 4 was stored in a Bessaneau Hangar, and the engine kept warm day and night by means of flameless lamps and covers. On December 17th, the machine was brought out for flight, and five gallons of hot water passed through the cooling system to take the chill off the metal. The draincock froze up after two gallons had passed through, and had to be taken out in order to allow the remainder of the water to be drained off. The engine was then filled with warm water and oil and gave 1,575 revolutions steadily for three minutes. Upon attempting to slow down the engine, it was found that the throttle barrel was frozen and could not be moved by the control. Upon removing the barrel it was noticed that the air intake pipes and mixing chambers were covered with ice an eighth of an inch thick, also the exhaust gas release from the induction heating system was frozen solid to a depth of three quarters of an inch, due to condensation on the pipe which runs to the edge of the outlet.

After the throttle barrel had been removed it was found that the controls were stiff due to freezing of the oil on the joints. All grades of lubricants were tried, and finally the best results were obtained by cleaning all lubricants off the joints and fulcrums and leaving them dry.

During this period there were several snowstorms. On December 23rd, the engine was started inside the hangar. It took twenty minutes to taxi to the "run-off" because of the loose snow on the road. The engine was giving 1,500 revolutions all the time, and the water was very hot. The pilot then tried to open out to take off and broke the control rods owing to the throttle being frozen again. The cowls were at once removed

> and it was found that the air intake pipe was
> coated both inside and outside with 1/4" of
> ice; the induction pipe and mixing chamber
> also had a coat of ice upon them, and the
> exhaust return from the induction heating
> system was frozen solid to a depth of 1".

Later, when this aircraft did succeed in taking off
it caught fire in the air, killing its pilot. Only
the Sopwiths, equipped with rotary motors, were
dependable during the winter months. The RE-8s
proved too heavy to carry bombs when equipped with
skis, which all landplanes required in order to make
safe landings and takeoffs.[12]

During the months of extreme temperatures and
overcast conditions flying was severely curtailed so
as not unnecessarily to risk the fragile machines and
the lives of the pilots. Therefore, the airplanes
were unavailable when Ironside decided to embark upon
a winter offensive along the railroad. Previously
operations in this area had been stymied by swampy
conditions. The freezing of the ground made the
advance feasible, at least in theory. The offensive
was designed so that American, British, and Russian
troops from Seletskoe would advance via the "Petrograd
Road" and drive the Bolsheviks from Kodish. At the
same time American and French troops on the railroad
would attack Plesetskaya thirty miles to the south.
It was expected that many prisoners would be taken,
that the Bolshevik fortifications would be destroyed,
and the enemy driven back at least fifty miles.
Ironside approved the plans for the offensive, but
even he admitted that it "failed miserably."[13]

On the railroad the plans of the Allies were
thwarted when the Bolsheviks unexpectedly, on the
afternoon of 30 December, opened a devastating
artillery barrage. "Their shelling was very good,"
noted Captain Eugene Prince, "and nearly hit our
armored train which was at v[erst] p[ost] 447 and
also they cut the Railway in four places." For the
next three days heavy and accurate shelling continued
until the American machine gunners were forced to
abandon their blockhouses. "Their battery of 4.2-inch
guns was particularly good," Prince reported, "and
they also displayed great knowledge of the location
of our blockhouses." The apparent explanation for
the debacle was that four deserters had alerted the
Bolsheviks to the forthcoming attack and had provided
detailed information about the Allies' defenses.[14]

Meanwhile the Allied operation against Kodish also
miscarried. The attacking force was to consist of two
American companies supported by a company of Russians

and a company of British troops. H. A. Doolittle of
the American embassy staff at Archangel personally
delivered the order to attack and witnessed the
ensuing battle. On schedule the Canadian artillery
began shelling Kodish at 6:00 a.m. on 30 December, but
only the American infantry advanced. As one American
soldier recorded in his diary: "Several men had their
feet frozen. Our force was to have been assisted by
the forces on the left and by the railroad. By some
unknown cause the forces did not participate in the
attack, therefore E, K, and part of the L Company had
all the work to do thus making it very hard for us."
The Russians--part of the same company that had
mutinied at Archangel--flatly refused to move. The
explanation from the Russian commander was that "it
was not the right kind of day" to fight. Furthermore,
the British column never appeared at all. In this
case it was stated that the British had reached a
point one and a half miles from Kodish but, hearing
no firing, concluded that the American attack had
failed and thus they returned to their original
position. In Doolittle's opinion, this version
seemed "very improbable" as there was heavy firing
the entire morning from artillery, machine guns, and
rifles from both sides.[15]

A subsequent investigation by Ironside discovered
the real reason for the fiasco: the intoxication of
Captain Gilbey, the commander of the British column.
Ironside's inquiry found that the preparations for
the attack were "totally inadequate and an important
detail such as small toboggans for drawing the Vickers
guns after leaving the sleighs was forgotten." In
removing the unfortunate officer from his command,
Ironside concluded there had been no valid reason for
abandoning the attack. Furthermore, wrote an enraged
Ironside, "The Russian platoon with him had done all
it was asked to do and the action of Captain Gilbey
was commented upon by the Russian officer in charge.
Such an example shown by a British officer in front
of Russian troops was nothing short of disgraceful."[16]

Surprisingly, the outnumbered Americans,
struggling through knee-deep snow, managed to drive
the 1,200 Bolsheviks of the Onega Regiment from
Kodish. Overnight the Bolsheviks received
reinforcements and on New Year's Eve they made a
determined effort to regain the town. Doolittle, who
witnessed the unsuccessful Bolshevik counterattack,
recorded that "the rattle of the machine gun and rifle
fire was practically continuous and in addition the
shouts of the Bolsheviks who were counter-attacking
and singing as they came could be easily heard.
Inasmuch as, from a civilian standpoint, things at

this moment were getting a bit thick, a strategic
retreat was carried out by the writer. . . ." The
assault on Kodish cost seven American lives, and after
holding the town for a week, subjected to constant
artillery fire, the Americans were forced to retreat
to their original position. Casualties might have
been even higher had not at least 20 percent of the
Bolshevik shells failed to explode. To Captain Prince
the experience demonstrated that "the Bolsheviks are
now well organized and offer stubborn resistance.
Their artillery fire has greatly improved in quality
and often their guns outrange ours and they do not
spare ammunition."[17] A similar inferiority in
artillery contributed to the embarrassing American
defeat at Shenkursk a few weeks later.

7

Defeat at Shenkursk

It was an accident of war that led the Allies to
select Shenkursk as their most advanced outpost
in North Russia. Originally General Poole had
intended to push as far south as Kotlas and Vologda.
The arrival of winter, Poole's removal as commander,
and the shift to a defensive strategy left the
Americans at Shenkursk in an isolated position that
was militarily unsound. Major General Aleksandr A.
Samoilo, a former Czarist officer who commanded
Soviet forces on the northern front, was quick to
note the vulnerable position of the Vaga column.
Accordingly, he planned in elaborate detail an
offensive to drive the Allies from Shenkursk and
destroy the garrison in the process. For the
operation he had available about 3,100 troops
compared to only 1,700 for the Allies, a figure
that included 400 Russian conscripts of dubious value
and loyalty. Samoilo counted upon superiority in
artillery and manpower to nullify the traditional
advantage enjoyed by the defense in winter fighting.[1]
     General Ironside was not ignorant of the
precarious location of Shenkursk. However, his
instructions were "to cut my coat according to my
cloth" and to withdraw from dangerous positions that
invited attack. As long as there was no military
pressure against Shenkursk, Ironside considered it
"out of the question" to withdraw. Furthermore,
sixty days of supplies had been stockpiled, and the
town and its outpost strongly fortified under the
direction of Colonel C. L. Graham, who in Ironside's
judgment was "a commander of great promise." Besides,
he noted, "I considered that my intelligence was good
enough to give me sufficient warning to operate a
successful evacuation in time to prevent our force
from being shut in." A further consideration in
Ironside's mind was that Shenkursk was the most

important city of the region except for Archangel,
and thus an evacuation without firing a shot would
have dealt a serious blow to the morale of the North
Russian government. "I therefore decided," concluded
Ironside, "to hold on as long as I could from a
military point of view in order to calm the minds
of the authorities."[2]

In retrospect, there were some warnings that
a Bolshevik offensive was imminent. Rumors of an
impending attack were widely circulated among
residents of Shenkursk. Bolshevik patrolling also
became more active near the American outpost of Ust
Padenga, eighteen miles southwest of Shenkursk. And
Allied intelligence did provide some warning of the
forthcoming assault. On 13 January, for example,
an Allied spy ("Agent S.I.S.") reported that the
Bolsheviks were awaiting the arrival of two fresh
regiments and that they intended to "operate on a
large scale" attacking simultaneously on all fronts,
including the American defenses on the Vaga. And on
16 January the Bolsheviks began a light shelling of
Ust Padenga.[3]

In Shenkursk itself all was quiet during the
Christmas season (celebrated by the Allies on
25 December and by the Russians thirteen days later).
The diary entries of Lieutenant Glen Weeks mentioned
"very good" singing by the Russian Y.M.C.A., a visit
to the local jeweler, card playing, reconstruction of
Shenkursk's fortifications, and extreme cold that
reached -27°. On Christmas day the Red Cross
presented each soldier with a stocking filled with
candy, dates, nuts, raisins, and cigarettes. For
dinner the menu featured roast beef, lamb, pork,
mashed potatoes and gravy, canned tomatoes, canned
peaches, and cake. After the meal "America" was sung
by the assembled multitude in the mess hall. And on
Christmas evening (as recorded by Edwin Arkins) the
Y.M.C.A. at Shenkursk presented a special program
including the following entertainments:

1. Russian stringed instrument.
2. Russian solo by young Russian woman.
3. Singer responds to encore with English
    song.
4. Violin and piano duet by American
    soldier, violinist and Russian lady
    pianist.
5. Russian stringed instruments.
6. "Down in Texas Town" by Russian teacher.
7. Song by Canadian Artilleryman, parody
    on "Way down South in Dixie."
8. Recitation by Canadian.

9. Violin and Piano duet.
10. Story by "Y" man.
11. Two songs by Russian soloist.
12. Song by Canadian Gunner.
13. Recitation in Russian by Cossack.
14. Song by Russian Cossack.
15. Russian National march.
16. Recitation "Casey at the Bat" by Co. C.
    man.
17. Song by Cossack.
18. Recitation by Canadian Sergeant.

On New Year's Day another special meal was served and
the troops celebrated by firing rifles and consuming
illegally acquired "gabby water."[4]
     Both Colonel Stewart and General Ironside visited
Shenkursk for the first time during this period.
Stewart was in the middle of a twenty-eight-day tour
in which he covered 600 miles by rail, horse, and
sleigh. According to Weeks, Stewart "gave the men
a fine talk." Later Stewart and the officers talked
in their quarters until midnight. "He left a very
good feeling with us," Weeks recorded. The next two
weeks were unusually uneventful. Weeks found his
time occupied with snowstorms, unloading convoys,
and trouble with an intelligence officer as a result
of "too much girl and not enough business." Typical
entries by Crissman and Arkins were "nothing new,"
"nothing materializes," or "nothing unusual." "Not
much change in conditions in general," noted Weeks on
17 January. The next day General Ironside arrived in
Shenkursk for an inspection and was thus present when
the Bolsheviks launched their surprise New Year's
offensive.[5]
     At 6:15 a.m. on 19 January 1919 Bolshevik
artillery, firing from a position that the Allies
were never able to locate, began to bombard the
American positions at Ust Padenga with three field
guns. About 7:30 a.m. the Americans were attacked
by 150 scouts dressed in white, supported by an
estimated 1,200 infantry. "And as fast as one of
them got nicked another one took his place," recalled
one officer. "Believe me, there were a hell of a lot
of 'em." In spite of what Ironside called "a gallant
resistance," the Americans and the Cossack infantry
"were driven in by force of numbers. All the Troops,
both Russian and American, did very well this day."
An estimated 150 casualties were inflicted on the
attackers, but the Americans were forced to evacuate
their outer posts and suffered heavy losses in the
process. Of the 43 Americans in the 4th Platoon of
Company "A" there were 32 casualties. "It's a real

war now," Sergeant John Crissman recorded in his diary.[6]

For three days heavy artillery fire continued as the Bolsheviks brought up a fourth field gun. Ironside estimated that the Bolsheviks fired 1,000 rounds on 19 January and 800 rounds on the days following. On the afternoon of 22 January, Graham ordered the evacuation of Ust Padenga and sent all available sleighs to assist in bringing out supplies and the wounded. During the afternoon the Bolsheviks launched an infantry attack that was repulsed by the Canadian Field Artillery. Under cover of darkness the Americans (at 1:10 a.m.) on 23 January evacuated Ust Padenga and headed for Shenkursk. "The Bolos were right after us," noted Crissman. "They opened artillery fire but could not locate us. We had to leave one piece of artillery on the road." So far bad weather had prevented the use of the airplanes at Beresnik. But on the 23rd, operating at a temperature of -30° Fahrenheit, the R.A.F. bombed the advancing Bolshevik columns. "Our aeroplanes cooperated successfully in the defence," Ironside recorded. Ordinarily 200-pound bombs would have been dropped from bomb racks. However, because of chronic problems with the release gear freezing in flight, each observer carried eight Cooper 20-pounders in his seat which were then dropped on the enemy by hand. Despite the use of electrically heated flying suits, several of the pilots were frostbitten.[7]

By the morning of 24 January the Americans had been driven back to Spaskoe, 2.4 miles southwest of Shenkursk. For the first time the Bolsheviks used two 4.2-inch howitzers and brought up 700 infantry who, in the opinion of Colonel Graham, "appeared quite fresh and well handled." At Spaskoe Captain Otto Odyard, who was regarded by Ironside as an "exceptionally fine" company commander, was seriously wounded in the neck by shrapnel. Captain O. A. Mowat of the Canadian Field Artillery was fatally wounded and one of the Canadians' eighteen-pounders was destroyed by shell fire. At 2:00 p.m. the Allied force retreated to Shenkursk which promptly came under siege. Private Edwin Arkins, while loading machine-gun belts at Shenkursk, recorded in his diary: "Shell hits Company billets breaking orderly room windows. Also hits Canadian Artillery stables knocking down one of the horses. Another shell hits building near billets setting it on fire. 'A' Company coming into Shenkursk while 'C' Company goes out to cover their retreat. 'A' Company man (Captain's orderly) is out of his head from shell shock. Machine guns and artillery can be heard on all sides of us."

In the opinion of Graham the situation was critical.
"The arrival of the 4.2-inch howitzers along with
Infantry reinforcements," he noted, "made it clear
that the enemy definitely intended to capture
Shenkursk, an operation he practically made certain
of by bringing up field howitzers, which the defence
were not capable of resisting. . . . Evacuation was
being considered but the possibility of getting clear
with a long convoy of wounded seemed very doubtful."[8]

In the meantime Ironside, who had returned to
Archangel by horse and sleigh, anxiously monitored
the battle reports. Although he "resisted sending
panic wires" to London, Ironside--with good reason--
was worried that the Vaga column would be "shut in
with no chance of relief." It was even possible, he
feared, that the Allies might be forced to abandon
Beresnik, where extensive stores of food and
ammunition had been stockpiled for the winter.
To avert such a disaster, Ironside asked for more
British troops, specifically requesting that two
battalions of infantry and a machine gun company
stationed at Murmansk be sent to Archangel. And
on the sixth day of the battle Ironside ordered the
entire Vaga column to retreat. "Seeing that the
enemy attacks were growing stronger and stronger and
that casualties had increased," Ironside reported,
"I ordered the evacuation of Shenkursk late on the
24th." The operation, he predicted, would not be
"an easy one" and would "of course have a great moral
effect." But Ironside felt he had no choice but to
abandon Shenkursk since he had few troops available
to organize a relief column. "The Bolsheviks on the
Dvina front," he concluded, "have been considerably
strengthened and have certainly been fighting better
than was to be expected."[9]

The evacuation order was delivered both by air
and by telegraph. Frank Shrive, a Canadian observer,
accompanied a Russian pilot from Beresnik to Shenkursk
to deliver Ironside's message. The pilot, who was
familiar with the area, noted that the Bolsheviks had
not yet occupied a little-used winter road. The trail
was usable only when frozen as it was too swampy to
be passable during the summer. Before communicating
the evacuation order to the Shenkursk command, it was
decided on the spur of the moment to bomb a nearby
Bolshevik gun position. On the second bombing run,
Shrive observed two Bolshevik soldiers open fire with
a machine gun and "in no time I felt the thud of
bullets on the machine." An attempt to return fire
was thwarted by the freezing of Shrive's Lewis machine
gun as the temperature still held at -30° Fahrenheit.
Only when the plane landed on the frozen Vaga River

at Shenkursk a few minutes later did Shrive realize
that the pilot had been seriously wounded by a bullet
that had penetrated his chest and lung. As it
turned out the evacuation order brought by Shrive
was unnecessary, since the message had been repeated
by telegraph and was acknowledged at Shenkursk just
before the Bolsheviks cut the wire to Beresnik.
Certainly, however, the news that an escape route
lay open was highly welcome.[10]

A daring night retreat was quickly organized by
Graham, who commented: "It would have been impossible
to have moved the convoy under the enemy's gunfire by
day and the secret withdrawal under cover of darkness
was considered the only chance as the place was
surrounded." First, seeking to give the impression
of preparing for a siege, Graham ordered all refugees
to leave the town by 3:00 the following morning. The
actual order to evacuate was not given until 9:30
p.m., after which the town gates were closed to
prevent anyone from leaving. "Every individual,"
read the orders, "is to be made to understand that
shouting, talking, or smoking during the night march
will endanger the lives of everyone in the column."
The main convoy departed at midnight, followed an
hour and a half later by 100 wounded Americans in
sleeping bags on sleighs. The primitive winter road,
pockmarked by "invisible horse hoof holes," was used
for the escape and 200 Bolsheviks who controlled the
main road with machine guns were avoided. "I keep
going," Arkins recorded, "by taking a swig of coffee
supplied us by the YMCA before leaving Shenkursk.
Have to break slush ice in mouth of canteen with
finger to reach coffee." During the march to
Shegovari, sixty miles away, many of the men threw
away their slippery Shackleton boots and marched
wearing multiple pairs of socks instead. Arkins
almost threw away his heavy sheepskin-lined overcoat.
However, he noted, "A Canadian artilleryman, seeing
my plight, offered to take it across his horse's
saddle. I threw it to him and was much relieved.
Real guys, those Canadians."[11]

In their retreat the Allies had to abandon all
their ammunition, most of their clothing and
equipment, and two of their eighteen-pound guns.
Supplies such as snowshoes and skis were smashed prior
to the retreat, but Graham decided not to destroy the
ammunition, since the resulting fires and explosions
might have revealed to the Bolsheviks that the Allies
were about to flee. As one soldier wrote his mother,
"We lost everything but the clothes on our backs. It
was a narrow escape. Down in the interior about three
hundred miles and if we hadn't got out that night we

would have been surrounded and all killed. It was
just a big miracle." Ironside basically concurred
in this judgment, noting that Graham had succeeded in
evacuating Shenkursk "in the nick of time." Forcing
the Allies to retreat seventy-five miles cost the
Bolsheviks an estimated 500 casualties, with many
of their wounded reported as having frozen to death.
Yet, the Shenkursk offensive demonstrated that the
Bolshevik army was an effective fighting force. In
the opinion of General Finlayson "the Bolshevik Army
on the Archangel Front is a well equipped, organised
and fairly well trained one." Graham also expressed
professional admiration, concluding: "I consider the
enemy troops well organized, well trained, and well
handled." And Ironside was also impressed by his
encounter with General Samoilo, conceding that the
Bolshevik general "had been very un-Russian and well
above the average of what we have encountered
hitherto."[12]

For two weeks the atmosphere remained tense
as the Bolsheviks probed with patrols and lobbed
artillery shells. Fortunately the Bolsheviks were
not as aggressive in their pursuit as in their
initial attack on Shenkursk. Twelve days of fighting
in subzero cold had taken their toll on Bolshevik
morale, and the heated buildings and foodstuffs
captured at Shenkursk proved an alluring attraction.
As John Cudahy commented: "When later the attacks
of February and March came, they were sporadic, and
lacked the fury, the sustained, and vehement driving
power of the first assault." By early February the
military pressure subsided as Allied planes reported
that the Bolsheviks had pulled back their troops and
artillery. On 7 February, for the first time since
the start of the Shenkursk offensive, Weeks was able
to change clothes and get a good night's sleep. Much
of the lieutenant's time was now taken up with letter
writing, playing dominoes and cards (black jack and
"chase the ace" were the most popular games), and
on 23 February his company played a game of baseball
in the snow against the Canadian artillerymen (losing
by the score of 21 to 5). Yet, from Ironside's
perspective, the American troops conducted too little
in the way of physical training and as a result the
"American troops deteriorated rapidly even from
the low value they already possessed, through the
incompetence of their officers in this portion of
their duties."[13]

Despite its relatively small scale, the Shenkursk
battle--fought within 300 miles of the Arctic Circle--
was the most extensive modern experience in winter
combat until the Russo-Finnish War of 1939 and the

German invasion of Russia in 1941. Ordinarily
during the North Russian fighting the defense had
enjoyed a substantial advantage. But in the Shenkursk
battle General Samoilo overcame the defenders through
the use of superior artillery and by exploiting a
two-to-one advantage in manpower. Both sides were
seriously hampered in their operations by frostbite
and the freezing of weapons. The Allies, in
particular, were prevented by intense cold and snow
storms from taking full advantage of their superiority
in the air. But in a sense the harsh conditions
aided the Allies in that the weather impeded Bolshevik
efforts to pursue the Allies after their withdrawal.
Curiously, however, neither side made any effort to
employ troops on skis, a tactic that often proved
effective during the winter campaigns of World War
II. No doubt the Bolsheviks should have won an even
more decisive victory than they achieved, as by
midnight on 24 January the Bolsheviks had surrounded
Shenkursk with three columns. Only Graham's risky
night retreat prevented the annihilation of the Vaga
column. Thus the Bolsheviks, despite winning a
psychological and tactical victory, failed in their
objective of capturing the garrison at Shenkursk and
driving the Allies from the Vaga valley. From the
Allied perspective the only positive result was that
the defeat suffered at the hands of Samoilo could
have been much worse.

8

A Crisis of Morale

In view of all the factors against them--enemy attacks, bitter cold and snow, long hours of duty and darkness, unappetizing food, the lack of reserves, and the unending nature of the conflict--it is hardly surprising that General Ironside's polyglot army experienced a severe crisis of morale. Much of Ironside's time and energy was now directed toward enforcing discipline and restoring morale among his disaffected forces. At Seletskoe on 22 February troops of the Yorkshire Battalion, newly arrived from Murmansk, disobeyed an order to occupy front line positions near Kodish. The Yorks demanded answers to such questions as "Why are we in Russia?" "Why are we fighting the Bolsheviks?" and "How long are we to remain?" News of the affair, which spread in exaggerated form with great rapidity among the Allied forces, came as a great shock to the British commander. "I had never in my life experienced a mutiny among British troops," Ironside recalled in his memoirs, "and I hated to think that the first signs of indiscipline should come from them, of all the Allied contingents." Two sergeants, the ringleaders of the affair, were placed under arrest, after which the remainder of the Yorks went forward and occupied the positions. After Ironside had addressed the men and observed their "hang-dog appearance," he telephoned Colonel Stewart and said, among other things, "The Yorks wanted to talk to Lloyd George about it."[1] Unknown to Stewart, he was soon to be placed in a similar position and required to quell a mutiny among his own troops.

The French were the next to rebel. On 1 March a French battalion, which was scheduled to relieve American troops on the railroad, mutinied at Archangel and, according to a note sent by Ironside to Colonel Stewart, "absolutely refused to go up."

The men took the position that Russians, not
Frenchmen, should occupy the front line. Accompanied
by the French military attaché, Ironside went to the
quarters of the rebellious battalion where he found
an attitude of determined intransigence. The
mutineers refused to stand up when the two men
entered their billet and they ridiculed the military
attaché when he appealed to their patriotism. As
a result Ironside found it necessary to disarm and
imprison 113 French soldiers. Hoping to head off the
spreading mood of disaffection, Ironside wrote to
Stewart: "A certain amount of talk has been going on
among the American Companies of not going back again
when their turn comes in 3 weeks or a month and know
you will do everything you can do to prevent such a
situation arising."[2]

Certainly Ironside's concern about the morale of
the 339th Infantry was well founded. As one injured
American noted after his return to America in April,
"A spirit of restlessness has been spreading over the
whole regiment since the armistice. No one has been
able to tell the men why they were fighting in Russia,
and naturally their morale was not what it should have
been." Dr. Arthur Nugent, a medical officer from
Milwaukee, Wisconsin, pointed out that the Americans
who fought Germany on the western front had no
difficulty in understanding their mission. "But we
were fighting a people against whom war had never
been declared and we didn't know why we were fighting
them." Under the circumstances, the 339th Infantry
felt forgotten and abandoned. The disillusioned
soldiers exchanged bitter remarks such as, "It's hell
to hang on, but it's death to stop," or "We are one
outfit that hasn't had to worry about finding jobs
after the war. We keep right on with what we are
doing."[3]

Critical letters detailing the shaky morale of
the troops began to filter through the heavy veil
of official censorship. Most of the letters were
smuggled out of Russia by wounded soldiers and then
printed in the Congressional Record or released to
the press by critics of the venture such as Senators
Charles E. Townsend of Michigan, Robert La Follette
of Wisconsin, and Hiram Johnson of California. The
letters he had received about conditions in North
Russia, said Senator Johnson, made "an American hang
his head in shame." One common theme was despair.
"This is the most Godforsaken country I have ever
seen," wrote a Milwaukee mechanic. "I'm full up
on Russia, and ready to move now," wrote another
Milwaukean. Others wrote of the disagreeable British
food ration: "All we got was canned willy [corned

beef] and hard tack." Not even the dogs would
touch the stuff, complained another soldier, and
he concluded: "We are living worse than a bunch of
hogs. You should see us. We are full of cooties,
dirty, ragged, no hair cut, no shave, and you should
see your ragged soldier now." The response of the
War Department was to order Colonel Stewart to
enforce censorship more effectively so as to prevent
the sending of letters "most unsoldierly in tone and
anti-British in sentiment."[4]

Above all, the American troops, like the Yorks,
asked why they were being ordered to fight the
Bolsheviks after the Germans, their original enemy,
had capitulated. A typical expression of discontent
was a typed statement entitled "Facts and Questions
Concerning the N.R.E.F." According to Colonel James
A. Ruggles of the American Military Mission, who
furnished a copy to Colonel Stewart, the document was
"written by an American officer with the Dvina force
and it is reported that it is widely circulated among
the American troops at the front and the men consider
that it fully covers their ideas regarding the reasons
why American troops are kept here." Stewart launched
an immediate inquiry seeking to discover the author
of the piece, but he "couldn't find out for sure."
The basic theme of the document was that the troops
should be sent home inasmuch as the original purpose
of the intervention--the defeat of Germany--had
long since been accomplished. Instead, "we are
now meddling with a Russian revolution and
counterrevolution." Moreover, "we have been unable
to reconcile this expedition with American ideals and
principles instilled within us." Anglophobia was also
much in evidence. The manner in which the British had
"mishandled" the expedition was termed "a disgrace to
the civilized world." Quoting an anonymous British
officer, the intervention was characterized as "an
effort to put on a show with two men and an orange."
Finally the author asked, "We wonder what propagander
[sic] is at work in the states, which enables the War
Department to keep troops here?"[5]

In America the War Department, while not actually
employing propagandists, sought to emphasize the
positive when releasing information on the Archangel
expedition to the public. Press reports based upon
War Department sources stressed that the American
forces were "bearing up splendidly," that "all
necessary equipment had been obtained and that
the comfort and welfare of the men [was] carefully
guarded." The health of the troops was described
as "excellent," morale as "very good," and the food
conditions as merely "good." Colonel Stewart was

quoted as saying that he had found "the general
health, discipline, and morale of the men excellent,
and their clothing and equipment ample." Stewart was
also reported as stating that the "troops were being
well taken care of in every way. . . and the Allied
command is capable of taking care of itself against
the whole Bolshevist army."[6]

Actually the War Department, in its press
releases, made a highly selective use of Stewart's
cables. Several of Stewart's statements concerning
the good health, discipline, and morale of the
American troops were excerpted from a report filed
on 7 January before the Bolshevik offensive at
Shenkursk. At the time of their publication in
America during the month of February these statements
were both out of date and misleading. On the other
hand, Stewart's cable of 17 February saying that the
troops were being well cared for and were ready and
able to defend themselves was accurately and promptly
published. By this time accounts of the Shenkursk
offensive and adverse living conditions had been
widely distributed. The purpose of Stewart's
reassuring telegram of 17 February, as its author
readily conceded, was to counter the effect of what
Stewart called "alarmist" and "highly exaggerated
reports." In publishing this cheery statement the
War Department omitted to mention that it had received
numerous complaints about Stewart's lack of leadership
and lack of sensitivity. Nor did the War Department
see fit to release Stewart's report of 3 February in
which he stated that the enemy was becoming more
numerous on all fronts. "The Allied command," the
worried colonel reported, "is small and we have no
reserves and are holding an outpost line from four
hundred miles in length and one hundred to two hundred
and sixty miles from Archangel." Ten days later
Stewart informed the War Department that his men, "due
to primitive conditions of life and continuous service
in the field under Arctic conditions," were "beginning
to feel the strain." And on 17 March Stewart pleaded
with his superiors to give him some information
concerning the possibility of relief so as to combat
the problem of declining morale.[7] Instead of trying
to reconcile the contradictions in Stewart's reports
the War Department, seeking to put its best foot
forward, selected the most favorable of the colonel's
statements for public release.

Still, most Americans had little if any awareness
of the North Russian campaign until the press carried
sensational accounts of a "mutiny" by American troops
at Archangel. According to the reports and a
subsequent press release by the War Department,

members of "I" Company, at the conclusion of a ten-day
rest period at Archangel, refused on 30 March to obey
an order to pack their equipment and return to the
railroad front. The troops asked questions such as
"Why are we fighting in Russia?" and "Why are we being
sent to the front now that the war on the Western
Front has ended?" The news was especially ominous
because an inspection report just a few weeks before
had characterized "I" Company as "undoubtedly the
strongest of the companies on this front." Captain
Horatio Winslow of Madison, Wisconsin, the commander
of Company "I," was the recipient of much unwanted
publicity. One Wisconsin newspaper ungraciously
speculated that Winslow had been subverted by
insidious socialist and Bolshevik propaganda.[8]
     Half an hour after learning of the trouble,
Colonel Stewart arrived and delivered a blunt
forty-minute lecture on the theme that he and the
nation expected every man to perform his duty as a
soldier. As recalled by Stewart, in a memorandum
written several months later, he appealed to the
soldiers' patriotism and sense of pride:

          I drew the attention of the company to
     the fact that their action was unprecedented
     in the history of the United States Army.
          I also invited their attention to the
     impression that would be created in the
     United States if they persisted in their
     conduct, so that it would be necessary for
     me to report the matter by cable to the
     United States, and asked them what their
     wives or mothers, fathers, sisters and
     brothers would think of them.

Following his talk Stewart answered questions. With
"some hesitation" one soldier questioned the sense
of fighting on behalf of a people who were "either
incapable or unwilling to help themselves."
Apparently the colonel's response was adequate since
when he asked whether any man present would now not
obey orders, none would come forward. The troops
then packed their equipment and marched to the railway
station. As Stewart recorded: "I mingled with the
men during this preparation and talked with many of
them regarding their equipment, service and other
matters and they all seemed in the best of humor and
spirits, and two of the platoons specially marched
off to the railway station singing."[9]
     All connected with the affair agreed that the
term "mutiny" was a distortion of what was basically
a trivial incident. One returning soldier recalled,

"We kicked like hell, but we didn't mutiny"; another called it "a case of shattered nerves, not mutiny." Major J. Brooks Nichols of Detroit regarded the incident as a misunderstanding and said, "I have heard more 'bunk' about this mutiny than could be written in a dozen books." Captain Winslow concurred stating, "There was no mutiny." A thorough investigation by Brigadier General Wilds P. Richardson confirmed that the incident was "of not a very serious character." In his view, the noncommissioned officers could have handled the affair more forcefully, but he commended Colonel Stewart for talking to the men and explaining the serious consequences of disobeying an order. Further action in the case "could not have served any good military purpose," Richardson concluded. However, DeWitt Poole, the American chargé at Archangel, regarded the incident as an object lesson and urged the State Department to announce a definite date for the withdrawal of the troops. To leave the 339th Infantry in Russia past the month of June was "quite out of the question."[10]

Fortunately, Stewart's appeal to "I" Company proved effective as, at that very moment, the presence of the troops was direly needed on the railroad front. Two weeks before, General Samoilo had launched a surprise spring offensive against the village of Bolshe Ozerke, which was strategically located between Onega on the White Sea and the town of Oberskaya on the railroad. During the winter months the road from Onega to Oberskaya had been the main route for transporting men and supplies from Murmansk to Archangel. Thus, Samoilo's immediate objective was to sever the link to Murmansk and then, if possible, seize Oberskaya and destroy the Allied force on the railroad. On paper the odds seemed to favor the Bolsheviks as they enjoyed a numerical advantage of about 7,000 troops to only 2,000 for the Allies. However, the soldiers Samoilo had available for the operation had been shipped only recently by railroad from the region of the southern Volga. They were not experienced in winter fighting and were deployed without the customary sheepskin coats and felt boots. Thawing conditions and deep snow banks, which soaked the clothing and feet of combatants on both sides, produced more cases of frostbite than there had been at any other time during the entire Archangel campaign. According to a conservative estimate, based upon Soviet sources, Bolshevik casualties totaled at least 2,000.

In the initial fighting the Bolsheviks easily carried the day. At Bolshe Ozerke, garrisoned by the French foreign legion, the 120 defenders were

overwhelmed by about 700 attackers led by Commander
Petr A. Solodukhin. Fearing that the Bolsheviks might
outflank the railroad from the west, Ironside assumed
personal command of the front. On 23 March Ironside
tried to retake Bolshe Ozerke with a two-pronged
offensive. Yet, the 700 British, American, and French
troops, exhausted by deep wet snow, were repulsed by
heavy machine-gun fire and suffered 75 casualties.
At the same time, however, the Bolsheviks were also
demoralized by deep snow drifts and by numerous cases
of frostbite that resulted from nighttime temperatures
as low as -22° Fahrenheit. Unable to retake Bolshe
Ozerke, Ironside leveled the town with artillery fire
on 25 March before returning to Archangel.[11]
     On 31 March a second phase of the spring offensive
began with an attack against the railroad front, whose
American defenders were by now well forewarned. At
8:30 a.m. the Bolsheviks cut the telephone line
between Archangel and the railroad troops. Half an
hour later three battalions of the Second Moscow
Regiment on skis attacked with machine guns in the
rear. The Americans responded with Lewis guns and
with point-blank fire from two three-inch artillery
pieces. Afterward nine enemy corpses were found on
the railroad and it was presumed that many additional
dead had been dragged off into the trees. A prisoner
testified that the Bolshevik attack had failed due
to the demoralizing effect of American artillery and
automatic-weapons fire. Heavy fighting continued
for two days as the 97th Saratov Regiment attacked
the front line, suffering an estimated 100 killed,
including its commander who was shot while riding
a white horse. "I" Company performed creditably
in the defense. "After they once got started from
Archangel," reported an observer, "they went up to
the front all right and they seem to be standing the
continuous shelling and the raiding that they have
had in the last 2 days pretty well."[12]
     Meanwhile, British forces on the railroad front
were also heavily engaged. On 2 April a company of
Yorks attempted a diversionary attack against Bolshe
Ozerke. However, the Yorks became lost in the woods
and their horses bogged down in deep snow. After an
inconclusive exchange of artillery and mortar fire
the exhausted and frostbitten Yorks retired to their
original position. And, on 5 April the British
stationed to the east of the railroad at Shred
Mekhrenga were attacked by a large Bolshevik force.
Three companies of Green Howards, firing from strongly
fortified blockhouses, repulsed the assault after
thirteen hours of fighting. Eighty prisoners were

taken and 100 corpses--victims of artillery fire--
were counted lying before the blockhouses.[13]

The end result of the spring offensive was a
continued stalemate, which again demonstrated the
enormous advantage possessed by the defense. Only
the original Bolshevik attack on Bolshe Ozerke,
accomplished with overwhelming numbers and complete
surprise, was a success. In the other battles it was
the defenders who prevailed. Apparently the strategy
of the Bolsheviks was militarily defective Since they
failed to coordinate their attacks against Bolshe
Ozerke and Oberskaya. As Ironside pointed out, "Had
the enemy attacked on the railway at the same moment
it is possible that the railway front would have
collapsed."[14]

9

The Americans Withdraw

Prior to the Paris Peace Conference it is doubtful
whether President Wilson directed much, if any,
attention to the unfolding of the Archangel
campaign. Even in the summer of 1918 he had found
it difficult to organize his thoughts on what policy
should be followed toward Russia. Only after a
painful mental struggle had Wilson agreed to
participate in the intervention while, in theory,
strictly limiting American forces to the role of
noncombatants. Understandably Wilson's mind in the
fall of 1918 was preoccupied with more pressing
matters such as the end of the war in Europe, the
congressional elections, and preparations for the
peace conference. But the president was familiar
enough with the British-led campaign in North Russia
to feel distinctly uncomfortable. In late November
Wilson agreed with Secretary of War Newton D. Baker
when he pointed out that American troops in North
Russia and Siberia were being used for purposes other
than those agreed to by the president. And Wilson
remarked in frustration that he found it "harder to
get out than it was to get in."[1]
   At the peace conference the president, reflecting
the caution he had consistently demonstrated in regard
to intervention in Russia, looked for ways and means
"to get out." First, Wilson in January 1919 sponsored
the ambiguous and ambitious Prinkipo Proposal whereby
the Allies invited all concerned parties to a
conference at Prinkipo in the Princes Islands near
Constantinople. Although the Bolsheviks responded
with enthusiasm, the plan faltered when Russian
anti-Bolshevik groups flatly rejected the idea.
President Chaikovsky of the Archangel government
played a prominent role in thwarting the conference,
contending that such a meeting would be immoral
and that reconciliation with the Bolsheviks was

impossible. William C. Bullitt, the American
diplomat who had originated the Prinkipo Proposal,
was so furious with Chaikovsky that he suggested
the moment had arrived for ending further American
support for the North Russian government. To prevent
a military disaster, he proposed withdrawing the
American troops by icebreaker. Although Colonel House
advised that Bullitt's idea was "worth considering,"
Wilson, for the time being, rejected a unilateral
American withdrawal, presumably because such a course
would be too harmful to American prestige and Allied
unity. Nevertheless, the President's desire to get
out of Russia continued undiminished. In mid-February
Winston Churchill, who had just replaced Lord Milner
as British secretary of state for war, advocated
sending arms and volunteers to anti-Bolshevik groups
in Russia. En route to America aboard his liner the
George Washington, Wilson cabled that he "would not
be in favor of any course contrary to that which may
mean the earliest practical withdrawal of military
forces. It would be fatal to be led further into
the Russian chaos."[2]

In announcing his decision to intervene in the
summer of 1918, the president had consolidated his
views in a complicated, lengthy document. This time
Wilson, harried by the demands of peacemaking and
domestic politics, declined to explain his views in a
formal statement. No doubt the president appreciated
that a unilateral American withdrawal announcement
would deeply offend the Allies, whose support he
needed on other issues at the peace conference.
Wilson found his solution by adopting an indirect,
but tactically adroit, strategy of withdrawal devised
by General Tasker Bliss. Shortly after the Allied
defeat at Shenkursk, Bliss had recommended the
approval of a British request for sending to Murmansk
two companies of American railroad troops to repair
the dilapidated Murman Railroad. Hurriedly
constructed during World War I, this route ran
southward from Murmansk toward Petrograd and was
occupied almost as far south as Lake Onega by British
forces under General Clarence Maynard. During the
winter months, when Archangel was closed by ice, the
Murman Railroad had served as a roundabout source of
supply from Europe. From the ice-free port of
Murmansk supplies would be shipped on the railroad
southward to Soroka. Then, because there was no rail
link between Soroka and Archangel, the supplies had
to be unloaded and laboriously transported by wagon
or sledge to Oberskaya where the road finally joined
the Archangel-Vologda Railroad.

Bliss argued that the repair of the Murman Railroad would help protect the American forces at Archangel in two ways: by making it possible to send them reinforcements and by providing a route for their withdrawal, if necessary. In approving the plan on 14 February, Wilson told Bliss that he should send copies to his British, French, and Italian colleagues on the Supreme War Council. Having carried out the president's instruction, Bliss triumphantly wrote Secretary of War Baker, "This, as I see it, commits us irrevocably to withdrawal of American troops the moment the weather conditions in the spring will permit. The sending of the railway companies in question will greatly facilitate their prompt withdrawal."

To Bliss this circuitous process was perfectly clear: it pointed the way toward withdrawal and avoided an open breach with the Allies. Baker concurred and on 18 February wrote a letter to the House and Senate Military Affairs Committees in which he communicated the president's decision to send the two railway companies to Murmansk. One of the purposes of the action, Baker explained, was "to facilitate the prompt withdrawal of American and Allied troops in North Russia at the earliest possible moment that weather conditions in the spring will permit." Baker's statement was published in the American Sentinel and thus it soon became common knowledge among the American troops in North Russia. But they and Colonel Stewart remained uneasy about their status and wondered why no official confirmation was forthcoming from Washington. What was perfectly clear to Wilson, Baker, and Bliss was anything but clear to the Americans marooned in the frozen Russian arctic.[3]

Protests at home from opponents of the intervention further impressed upon the Wilson administration the wisdom of extricating itself from what the president had termed "the Russian chaos." Led by Senator Hiram Johnson of California, isolationist critics assailed Wilson for having submitted to a de facto league of nations by accepting British command over the Americans in North Russia. "Under the orders of foreign nations Americans wage war without declaration by the American Congress or the consent of the American people," he charged. Johnson caused Wilson additional embarrassment when, on 14 February, he almost succeeded in getting through the Senate a resolution demanding the withdrawal of the 339th Infantry. The vote ended in a tie and the ballot of Vice President Thomas R. Marshall was required to defeat it. Governor E. L. Philipp of

Wisconsin, the home state of 500 troops sent to North Russia, also demanded an immediate pullout. "Our country is not at war with Russia and we should not keep an army in that country," he stated. "I am in favor of withdrawing our army at once." In fact, Wilson had already taken concrete steps to withdraw unilaterally. A few weeks previously Brigadier General Wilds P. Richardson, an officer with Alaskan experience, had been appointed to command the American forces in Russia and to supervise their evacuation. When Richardson met the president at Paris in mid-March to discuss his assignment, Wilson was emphatic in criticizing the British use of the American forces and stated that he desired the withdrawal of all Americans "as soon as practicable after the opening of navigation."[4]

Independently the British reached a similar conclusion. On 4 March the War Cabinet, on practical grounds, decided to terminate the British presence in North Russia. From a military standpoint it was felt that North Russia was now of less importance than Siberia and southern Russia. Moreover, a continuation of the campaign using drafted troops was viewed as politically untenable. To replace the exhausted conscripts, the War Office announced a drive to recruit 8,000 volunteer soldiers and aviators who were supposedly to be used only for defensive operations. Launched at a time when civilian employment was in short supply, the campaign was a complete success. For the time being it was decided to keep the decision to withdraw a secret from the Archangel government.[5]

For months following their arrival at Archangel the Allies had nurtured the pleasant notion that the "Provisional Government of the Northern Region" was a democratic government enjoying broad popular support throughout the region. The Allied ambassadors, who had little else to do, spent much of their time offering free advice to Poole and Chaikovsky. Gradually, as the ambassadors returned to the West (Francis left in November and Noulens a month later), the original emphasis upon preparing the region for democracy faded. The prestige of the government also declined when Chaikovsky, apparently bored with his role as a figurehead, departed from Archangel in January to attend the Paris Peace Conference. Technically Chaikovsky retained the title of president, but the real power lay in the governor-general and foreign minister, General Eugene K. Miller, a fifty-one-year-old professional soldier and native of the Baltic region. Under Miller the government was more a military dictatorship than a

democracy; militarily and financially it was
dependent upon the Allies for its very existence.[6]
    From Ironside's perspective, Miller, despite
tendencies to issue bombastic proclamations and to
waste time on unimportant paper work, was a decided
improvement over Chaikovsky and Samarin. Ironside
was especially pleased with the apparent progress
made by Miller in mobilizing the Russian National
Army. By the beginning of April, 14,000 partially
trained troops were available. Russian officers were
in very short supply and therefore Ironside found
it "was necessary to make the best of even the most
unpromising material." Much of the training was
supervised by British officers who emphasized
physical training as a means of preserving morale
during the long winter months. Pronouncing the
mobilization "an enormous success," Ironside
optimistically concluded: "I think it shows the
greatest example of what good British officers. . .
can do with good material in a short time and under
great difficulties owing to lack of interpreters."
Ironside was almost as optimistic concerning the
3,875-man Slavo-British Legion. Originally organized
by Poole, this group had been de-emphasized by
Ironside in favor of building the Russian National
Army. However, as the fighting progressed large
numbers of captured Bolshevik soldiers, deserters,
political prisoners, and common criminals became
available at the Archangel prison. Seeing that these
groups were not suitable candidates for the Russian
National Army, Ironside accepted their enlistment in
the Slavo-British Legion. On the parade ground the
showing of these units was impressive. The acid test
of their loyalty and effectiveness did not come until
they were sent to the front to complete their
military training.[7]
    To the great relief of the demoralized and
fatigued Allied forces, the expected all-out
Bolshevik spring offensive on the Dvina failed to
materialize. Theoretically the April thaw should
have given the Bolsheviks a decided advantage as the
river ice disintegrated upstream first, presenting
the Bolsheviks with a golden opportunity to attack
with gunboats while the Allied vessels were still
icebound at Archangel. To avert such a catastrophe,
the British dispatched the S.S. Wargrange to Archangel
with DH-9As, Sopwith 1 1/2 Strutters, and six Short
184 seaplanes. The idea was to attack the Bolshevik
gunboats while they were still frozen in the Dvina
at Kotlas. However, the plan miscarried when the
Wargrange became marooned in the frozen White Sea and
did not reach its destination until after the breakup

of the ice. A further worry for the Allied commanders was that the spring thaw temporarily immobilized the Allied planes already in North Russia by covering the flying fields with up to six inches of water. In mid-April, when the skis were removed from two of the Sopwiths at Oberskaya, the ground was too soft to permit a takeoff; according to Frank Shrive, "a seaplane would have had more success." However, drainage ditches were dug and within a few days the field was once again usable. Not until 25 April did the Bolsheviks attempt to put their gunboats into action against the well-prepared British and Russian defenders. Between the efforts of the planes and sixty-pound guns manned by Russians, the Bolshevik gunboats were kept at bay.[8]

Ominously, however, the performance of the Russian troops was unreliable. Twice during the spring the Russians mutinied. The most serious trouble occurred at Tulgas on 25 April when 300 Russians murdered their officers and deserted. A less serious incident of disaffection took place at Pinega on 14 May where two officers were shot in a pay dispute. To restore discipline Ironside ordered the execution of fifteen malefactors. "In each case," Ironside reported, "the real cause was the lack of administrative ability on the part of the Authorities and Regimental officers. The Government allowed the pay to fall into arrears, and the officers failed to understand that when not fighting they had to occupy themselves with their men in training and recreation. Like all troops, Russian troops become discontented if left long in idleness." Ready or not, Ironside felt he had no alternative except to send the Russians into the field as replacements for the departing Allied troops.

Even though the loyalty and fighting ability of the White Russians were dubious, the Bolsheviks came out of the winter in even worse condition. On the Dvina front hundreds of deserters surrendered at the end of April, and Ironside found that "all were in miserable condition, badly fed and clothed, and all indescribably dirty." Optimistically, Ironside felt that with continued training on the British model the freshly organized troops could be shaped into an effective fighting force. But he overlooked the example set during the Shenkursk campaign when newly mobilized Russian troops had proved to be highly susceptible to Bolshevik propaganda. Of necessity Ironside was forced to base his hopes on a weak reed.[9]

On the Dvina the spring thaw had been the signal for renewed skirmishing. Elsewhere the country was a quagmire, which effectively ruled out offensive action by either side. On the railroad the main occupation

of the troops was to repair the track which was
described as being in "very bad condition" after
the thawing of the snow. Frequently, noted one
observer, the locomotive engineers were forced
to slow their trains "to a walking pace to avoid
drowning of the train and crew in the swamps on
either side of the track." The Bolsheviks also had
problems in maintaining the track and equipment under
their control. In late April Captain J. A. Harzfeld
was permitted to cross to the Bolshevik side of the
railroad front and travel to Vologda in order to
return an American prisoner of war who was exchanged
for four Bolsheviks. After a two-hour dinner in the
private car of the Soviet commander of the railroad
front, Harzfeld proceeded by rail to Vologda, a
journey that required twenty hours to cover 400 versts
(265 miles). During his five days at Vologda he was
permitted "complete freedom of movement," and observed
bustling rail traffic and an abundance of rolling
stock, most of which was in need of repair. But, in
Harzfeld's opinion, the repair facilities at Vologda
no longer were able to perform competently as the
refurbished car on which he returned to the front
had three flat wheels.[10]

For the American troops the railroad war came
to a virtual end in the third week of April. Then
Ironside informed the new American commander, General
Richardson: "I propose to withdraw all the American
Infantry from the Railway Line by the second week in
May. It will not then be the intention to employ them
in the field again." To transport the troops to
Archangel only two woodburning locomotives, which
frequently broke down, were available. Top speed was
limited to twenty miles per hour, and with stops the
100-mile trip from Oberskaya to Archangel required
several hours. Despite the low speeds, travel on
the railroad was a surprisingly hazardous experience.
On 25 May thirty-five Americans were injured and one
killed when a British train running backward was
mistakenly switched onto a siding where it struck box
cars filled with engineers. One soldier from Detroit
had both legs broken and his right hand was so badly
mangled it had to be amputated.[11]

The prospect of leaving Russia did wonders for
morale as did the arrival of spring, accompanied by
round-the-clock daylight. On 13 May the Canadian
aviator Frank Shrive recorded in his diary,

> Mentioned some time back that this
> railroad runs true north and south. Last
> night it was as clear as a bell and towards
> ten-thirty the sun dipped down just to the

left of the track. Mac and I watched as it
disappeared. We then decided to get some
beer from the Mess and come out and watch
it come up. Almost right on the dot at
one-thirty and at about the same distance to
the right of the track it came into view.
Of course even at midnight it never did get
dark.

The chief worry of the Americans was no longer the
Bolshevik armored train, but how to win the baseball
championship of North Russia. To the exasperation
of the R.A.F., the Americans insisted on using the
airfield at Oberskaya for baseball practice. It
took several low passes by a Sopwith Camel before
the Americans were persuaded to take their game
elsewhere.[12]

On the Dvina the American withdrawal got under
way a month earlier than on the railroad. "Everything
looks as if we are on the way home," noted John
Crissman in his diary on 5 April. "Other companies
from front are moving toward Archangel." At Beresnik
Crissman was "billeted in an old barn which was
formerly a morgue." At least he was able to take a
bath, have his clothes deloused, wonder at the novelty
of electric lights, see a movie, and attend a minstrel
show. Stationed a few miles upstream, Edwin Arkins
recorded the arrival of much warmer weather, slush,
muddy roads, and "very poor" sanitary conditions.
"Nothing unusual," was one of Arkins's most frequent
observations. In the evening the troops were often
entertained by improvised talent shows of minstrels
and singers. "One of the main attractions," recorded
Arkins, "was an instrument made out of hard tack can,
M. & V. can and cornbeef can and a piece of wood made
similar to a banjo. Produces very good music."[13]

Likewise the diary of Glen Weeks, which had
previously contained detailed accounts of fire fights,
now dealt with such matters as melting snow, fishing,
duck hunting, card playing, two fighting roosters
falling into a well, and the court-martialing of
several of his men to determine where they had got
their liquor. A woman presented Weeks with two dogs
that were appropriately named Lenin and Trotsky.
Retreating toward Archangel Weeks laconically noted:
"We burned the mill in the woods outside of Shuskega,"
and on 2 May he recorded: "Beautiful day. . . .
Gunboats bombarded Kurgomen. Burned the two churches.
We took a couple of prisoners; also arrested a family
caught signalling to the Bolo gunboats. They had
a dance at the Y. I wrote a couple of letters in
the evening." By late May the main subject of the

diarist's concern was how to defeat the Canadian
artillerymen at baseball. Unfortunately, in the
last inning "our men went to pieces and the Canadians
beat us." A rematch was aborted when the baseball
refused to stay in one piece. Meanwhile, the American
headquarters at Archangel, no longer fearful of being
driven into the sea, busied itself with harassing
soldiers for such infractions of military decorum as
being improperly shaven or failing to salute, or for
appearing in public with their coats or blouses dirty,
ripped, or unbuttoned.[14]

Finally at 5:30 p.m. on Saturday 7 June, Weeks
and his troops arrived at Archangel by boat and eight
days later, dodging large ice floes in the White Sea,
the transports Menominee and Porto evacuated all but
a small rear guard of the American North Russian
Expeditionary Force. But not even the withdrawal
erased the Americans' latent feelings of bitterness.
Due to misinformation as to the sailing time of the
Porto, Ironside arrived too late to thank the 339th
Infantry in person for their efforts. As a good
politician, Ironside took pains to assure Colonel
Stewart that the incident was not intended as a
snub. "I am afraid I have mixed things up properly,"
Ironside apologized. Presumably the departing troops
should have been grateful for the generous supply of
medals conferred upon them by British headquarters.
But General Richardson, for one, was not at all
impressed. He sensed condescending overtones of
British imperialism in the copious awarding of
decorations and suggested that the 339th Infantry
had been treated in the manner of colonial forces
from Africa or India. The policy of making liberal
awards, he contended, "has been done apparently in
much the same manner as the distribution of gifts
by masters to their slaves in the South, in the
ante-bellum days. In other words, it is accompanied
throughout by a spirit of superiority on the part
of the donors which, although perhaps not intended,
nevertheless cannot be concealed. This has become
a traditional spirit in the British Army through
generations of handling troops of inferior races."[15]

During a brief stopover at Murmansk, described
by one observer as a "dirty town of shack buildings,"
the troops experienced their last taste of combat.
Unwisely the Menominee was docked opposite an
incoming British troopship bringing reinforcements
to Archangel. Among the British volunteers the story
was rife that the American performance in Russia had
been mutinous and cowardly. "Why was it that the
Yanks turned tail at Ust Padenga?" was a question
often addressed to Ralph Albertson. What began as

mere "ribald banter" between British sailors and
American soldiers soon degenerated into an exchange
of insults. According to a British pilot who
witnessed the affair, it was the Americans (objecting
to being called "bloody hobos") who began throwing
lumps of coal. Before the pilot "could say 'Jack
Robinson' buckets of coal were being handed up from
below at amazing speed." Numerous casualties were
recorded on both sides, but it was the British,
throwing bottles in addition to coal, who took the
honors. "I saw one Yank take an enormous lump full
in the face," recorded the British observer. "One of
our men is hit by bottle thrown from opposite ship,"
Edwin Arkins noted in his diary. Finally, one of the
Americans "committed a dastardly act," by throwing
an open jackknife that missed its target. Such
cowardice, maintained pilot Ira Jones, explained
the Americans' "unenviable war record in Russia."
The remainder of the trip was far less eventful.
On 26 June the Menominee arrived at Brest, and five
days later Lieutenant Weeks and members of the 339th
Infantry sailed for America on the S.S. President
Grant.[16]

10

From Optimism to Despair

The first ten months of the Allied intervention in
North Russia (August 1918-May 1919) were marked by
a pattern of initial buoyant optimism followed by
abject despair. On a lesser scale the final four
months of the British presence repeated the pattern.

A mood of elation was briefly established by
the arrival at Archangel on 26 May of four troop-
carrying transports escorted by the American cruiser
Des Moines. On board was Grogan's Brigade, named
after its commander, Brigadier General G. W. St.
G. Grogan, winner of the Victoria Cross, an award
comparable to the American Congressional Medal of
Honor. When the troops disembarked the following
day they were greeted by sunshine and the pealing
of church bells and were welcomed by General Miller
who presented platters of bread and salt. A crowd
estimated by Ironside to number 20,000 demonstrated
its approval, although Ironside noted with irritation
that approximately 3,000 able-bodied men were present
who had apparently escaped being drafted into the
Russian National Army. Additional enthusiasm greeted
the arrival of the second contingent of British
volunteers on 10 June under the command of Brigadier
General L. W. de V. Sadleir-Jackson. He was escorted
by a refurbished naval flotilla under Captain E.
Altham, a veteran of fighting on the Dvina the
previous fall. Upon the arrival of the reinforcements
the evacuation of all British troops who had spent the
winter in North Russia was commenced.[1]

Likewise in London there was great, but mistaken,
optimism that the White Russians would finally prevail
over the Bolsheviks. Admiral Aleksandr Kolchak, the
White leader in Siberia, appeared well positioned in
the spring of 1919 to establish a military link with
Archangel. That such a junction was feasible was
apparently demonstrated in late March when a group

of twenty volunteers managed to cross the 400 miles
separating the North Russian and Siberian forces.
Prime Minister David Lloyd George was primarily
concerned with the deliberations of the Paris Peace
Conference and gave only sporadic attention to
implementing the evacuation policy decided upon by
the War Cabinet on 4 March. However, several members
of his government, especially Winston Churchill and
General Henry Wilson, were quick to see the military
and political advantages of delaying the evacuation
until the winter of 1919 so as to leave the White
Russians in as strong a position as possible.
Britain might then disengage with honor and,
presumably, criticism of those who had advocated the
intervention in the first place would be minimized.[2]

General Wilson, not dismayed by Poole's experience
the previous fall, advocated sending Ironside with his
new troops and flotilla on an offensive against Kotlas
to join up with Kolchak. His only intent, Wilson
argued, was to strike a disengaging blow against the
Bolsheviks and to facilitate a union of the forces of
North Russia with Kolchak. Wilson flatly rejected as
"moonshine" any insinuation that his real purpose was
to promote an escalation of the fighting rather than
carry out the avowed policy of withdrawal. Churchill
was likewise an enthusiastic proponent of offensive
operations against the Bolsheviks. It was he who had
originated the plan for sending the two British relief
brigades to Archangel. He also flirted with various
schemes for attacking Petrograd with a combined
Finnish-German force supported by the Royal Navy.
Equally fantastic was Churchill's proposal whereby
30,000 Czechs would be encouraged to fight their way
from Siberia to Archangel. Although Churchill was
able to get Cabinet approval of the plan, the Czechs
showed no interest in the idea, preferring to be
repatriated instead through Vladivostok.

Beginning in June, however, discouraging news
from both Siberia and Archangel considerably
diminished the earlier mood of optimism. In the
first place, it was learned on 12 June that Admiral
Kolchak had suffered a crushing reverse in Siberia,
a setback that effectively doomed any hope that the
White Russians would be able to advance to Kotlas.
Foreign Secretary Curzon, who presided over the
War Cabinet while Lloyd George completed the final
details of the Versailles Treaty, began to question
the wisdom of the planned Dvina offensive. He felt
no lasting purpose would be served in capturing
Kotlas unless the forces of Kolchak were able to
arrive there also. And he pointed to the strong
opposition by British unions to a military campaign

in Russia. For the time being, Churchill and General
Wilson, the optimists in the cabinet, carried the
debate by emphasizing that the attack against Kotlas
was necessary in order to permit the unimpeded
evacuation of British forces.[3]

On paper the planned offensive was highly
ambitious. The main advance on the Dvina was to
be preceded by mine-sweeping operations carried out
by the naval flotilla supported by airplanes from
Beresnik. Meanwhile, Russian troops on the railroad
would capture Plesetskaya, a goal that had previously
eluded both Poole and Ironside. On the river British
and Russian troops would drive the Bolsheviks from
Pinega and Kotlas. If all went according to plan, the
Bolsheviks would be deprived of winter bases and the
British would be able to disengage, leaving the North
Russians in a strong defensive position. Perhaps the
forces of Kolchak would be so encouraged that they
would join the North Russians at Kotlas after all.[4]

Privately, however, Ironside had serious doubts
as to whether he could achieve such a military coup.
Certainly the past performance of the Russian troops,
who were counted upon to do the bulk of the fighting,
did not inspire confidence. Another consideration
that had to be taken into account was the adverse
weather. This time the problem was constant daylight
and drought. The water level of the Dvina steadily
receded, until on 9 July the river reached an all-time
low. In the words of a "narrative of events" drawn
up by the War Office: "This immobilized the Naval
flotilla and rendered its co-operation in operations
up the river impossible and, moreover, upset all
arrangements for the river transport of the force."
Nevertheless, Ironside did have the use of two
gunboats when he ordered Graham to undertake a modest
advance up the Dvina on 20 June. The objective was
to capture high ground used by the Bolsheviks for
observation posts in the vicinity of Troitsa and to
sweep mines from the river. On this occasion the
troops of the Russian National Army performed
satisfactorily; however, British troops under the
command of Lieutenant Colonel John Sherwood-Kelly
failed, either due to a misunderstanding or a loss
of nerve, to participate. Four hundred prisoners and
three field guns were captured, and several Bolshevik
barges were damaged or sunk. Still, considering the
demoralized and famished state of the Bolsheviks,
Ironside felt the offensive "had not been as
overwhelming a success as it should have been."[5]
The month of June thus ended with a mood of mild
disillusionment, only to be followed in July by a
descent into despair.

Mainly responsible for the collapse of British confidence was a determined mutiny that occurred at Troitsa on 7 July in Ironside's pride and joy, the Slavo-British Legion. The shock was especially great because there was no suspicion at all that trouble was brewing. According to the official report, eight mutineers from Dyer's battalion, named in honor of a Canadian officer who had commanded the group prior to his death, broke into the officers' quarters at 2:30 a.m. and shot to death five British and four Russian officers. "Not content with this," recorded Ira Jones, "they tore their intestines open with knives and bespattered their faces with them." The eight ringleaders, armed with revolvers, then compelled or convinced more than 200 of the troops to flee to the Bolshevik lines. Only half an hour before, a Russian officer had visited the officers' billets and found everything to be quiet. The murderers, until the moment of the crime, escaped suspicion, having established reputations as "some of the best behaved and most efficient soldiers in the Battalion."[6]

By barge Ironside traveled to Troitsa to investigate. His decision was to disarm the Dyer's battalion, except for a machine-gun company that was considered to be loyal. Most of the battalion was converted into a labor company and sent back to Archangel. None of the ringleaders was apprehended, but as an example Ironside decided to execute "about 20" who were caught trying to reach the Bolshevik lines. When the War Office protested the shooting of so large a number, Ironside compromised by executing just eleven. The sentences were carried out on 20 July by members of the Slavo-British Legion who had not mutinied and who were themselves covered by machine gunners of the 45th Royal Fusiliers. Ira Jones witnessed the ensuing drama that consisted, he said, of three acts,

Act 1. The prisoners--thirteen in all-- were in tents and a priest went to bless them and take any messages to relatives. Each one was sprinkled with Holy water, and the priest kissed each one. Act 2. The prisoners were marched under escort to the place of execution, where Russian and English troops formed three sides of a square, the other side being taken by spectators. The doomed men were placed in a row with their backs to the place of execution and their sentences read out. Two were reprieved and sentenced to imprisonment. Act 3. Those to be shot were blindfolded and the stripes of a fine-

looking sergeant were torn off his coat
sleeves. Each man was then taken by the arm
by British soldiers and led to posts where
they were tied arms and feet. A disc was
placed on their breasts opposite their
hearts, as a target. Some of the cowardly
ones cried hysterically, but the sergeant
was a real stoic. . . . The signal to fire
was when the Russian officer dropped his
upraised sword. There was a hush when he
lifted his sword, then a strange thing
happened which lengthened the lives and
agony of those Bolos for about one minute.
A little dog appeared from somewhere and
trotted up to one of the prisoners and
sniffed at his legs. The dog had to be got
away before the officer dropped his sword.
I shall never forget the rattle of those
machine-guns and the wriggling bodies as
their life was shot out of them. The
executioner of the sergeant, either
deliberately missed him or became very
nervous, because when the smoke of the guns
cleared away the N.C.O. had pulled off his
handkerchief and was shouting 'Long live
Bolshevism.'

The survivor was dispatched with pistol shots and the
corpses buried in a mass grave that the condemned men
had themselves dug several hours before. Jones saw
the two reprieved men being marched to confinement
and "it was obvious they had made a mess in their
trousers. In similar circumstances I suppose I would
do the same," Jones observed.[7]
     Prior to the mutiny of the Slavo-British Legion,
Ironside had assumed, at least outwardly, an attitude
of confidence. He had maintained that it was his
duty as a soldier to overcome whatever obstacles
were placed in his path. From now on, though, he was
hardly able to conceal his discouragement. General
Marushevsky, who urged Ironside to push up the Dvina
to Kotlas, observed that the British commander had
become withdrawn and morose. In fact, Ironside's
patience was wearing thin. From a tactical standpoint
he felt a disengaging blow was essential to permit
the British to evacuate and leave the Russians in
a strong defensive position. But he was extremely
dubious of trying to advance deep into the interior
despite the assurances of Miller and Marushevsky that
the inhabitants would rise in support of the Allied
cause. On the contrary, Ironside reported, "My own
experience is that population does not join willingly

and always sits on the fence." He would leave the
Russians sufficient food for the winter but that was
all. No British troops or even a British military
mission should stay. In a handwritten outline,
in which he consolidated his thoughts, Ironside
reasoned that a continued military presence would
lead to embarrassing questions in the House of
Commons, and would merely encourage the Russians
to continue leaning on Britain for support. In a
nutshell, Ironside's view was: "(a) No British
troops; (b) No mission unless remainder of Russia
admits of it." And, to the War Office he bluntly
stated his disillusionment: "I personally do not
think after what we have done for Russia that we now
owe them anything and that we should set our faces
against evacuating any but Allies. They are not
worth fighting for if they do not stand up."[8]

Two days after writing this gloomy assessment
Ironside was compelled to report another major
mutiny. This time the trouble broke out at Onega
where mutineers at 1:00 a.m. on 20 July handed over
the entire area to the Bolsheviks. Even Ironside
conceded that his bright hopes for the Russian troops
had been shattered. As he admitted to the War Office:
"State of Russian troops such that it is certain my
efforts to consolidate Russian National Army are
definitely a failure. As early evacuation as
possible essential now unless British force here
is to be increased." It was Ironside's opinion that
the withdrawal should be carried out as a "complete
military evacuation" with the destruction of all
military supplies of any use to the Bolsheviks. He
also proposed to issue a blunt proclamation to the
population at the moment the evacuation began. In
no uncertain terms this document stated what Ironside
proposed to do and what were the consequences of
opposing him:

> I have been appointed Military dictator
> of the Archangel region occupied by Allied
> forces. I am disarming the Russian National
> Army of the Northern region and dismissing
> men to their homes. I am withdrawing Allied
> forces to Archangel and will embark them
> there for evacuation.
> I warn you that if you attempt to
> interfere with this evacuation I shall
> employ the full force of Army and Navy
> against you and will deal ruthlessly with
> all agents committing acts against law and
> order.

> I am setting up in Archangel a temporary
> local Authority chosen by the community with
> which you may deal when I have evacuated the
> town.
>
> No executions of prisoners in my hands
> will take place from the date of my assuming
> dictatorship.
>
> I am prepared to exchange all prisoners
> held by me prior to evacuation against all
> British subjects held by you.
>
> I shall evacuate these prisoners as
> hostages should you not agree to this.[9]

The next day (29 July) the War Cabinet made up
its mind once and for all to withdraw from North
Russia as soon as possible. Ironside was authorized
to assume the status of military dictator "from any
date you consider desirable." But he was specifically
forbidden to negotiate an armistice with the
Bolsheviks "as this would have the worst possible
effects on the other fronts and compromise the
political situation." Ironside's hard line advice not
to evacuate civilians was overruled on humanitarian
grounds and he was told to prepare to transport "all
Russians and others who want to go" up to a total of
13,500. All military stores that could not be removed
were to be destroyed to deny them to the Bolsheviks.
The remaining food supplies were to be distributed
over as wide an area as possible. Finally, the War
Cabinet accepted the recommendation of General Wilson
to appoint a senior officer, General Sir Henry S.
Rawlinson, to supervise the evacuation. Accompanied
by three tanks, two machine-gun battalions, an
infantry battalion, and a field ambulance group,
Rawlinson hurriedly departed from Newcastle on
4 August on the steamer _Czaritsa_.[10]
In the meantime, as wild rumors of the impending
evacuation circulated throughout Archangel province,
Ironside twice met with members of the Archangel
government (on 27 and 28 July) and confirmed for
the first time that no British troops or ships would
remain during the winter. He did not, however, reveal
that he planned to complete the process by 1 October
and left the impression that the withdrawal would not
be completed for at least another month. After a long
debate the members of the government took the position
that they had little chance of holding the region
without British military support. But they denied
any intention of surrendering, telling Ironside "that
they considered it their duty to continue after our
departure to fight for the good of the common cause
that of defeating Bolshevism."[11]

Two questions remained to be decided: the timing of the long-contemplated disengaging blow, and the composition of the attacking force. Personally Ironside, who had lost all confidence in the Russian troops, preferred to exclude them from the operation entirely. In his opinion it was "very doubtful" whether the Russians would fight at all. And even if they did agree to participate the result could only be an "inevitable disaster." But General Miller had his heart set on an immediate offensive by Russian soldiers as the only means to restore morale. Also General Rawlinson favored an immediate attack to break the Bolshevik front and permit an evacuation before the enemy could recover. "In my opinion," cabled Rawlinson, "it will be necessary to give the enemy a good hard knock either just before or very soon after withdrawal from our present forward positions begins." Ironside then flew by seaplane to consult with General Sadleir-Jackson, who commanded the Dvina front. Concluding that his plans were both bold and meticulous Ironside ordered the offensive to begin on 10 August. Meanwhile, Ironside returned to Archangel to report to Rawlinson.[12]

In the resulting campaign 3,000 troops advanced twenty miles and in the process shattered the defenses of an estimated 6,000 Bolsheviks. Soon more than 2,000 prisoners were "in the cages"; eighteen guns and numerous machine guns were also captured. An estimated 500 of the enemy were killed, 800 wounded, and about 300 incapacitated by 600 gas shells, the firing of which took the Bolsheviks completely by surprise. Despite the low water in the Dvina, the naval flotilla was able to assist the advance by sweeping mines and shelling. Additional help was furnished by a rejuvenated Royal Air Force contingent at Beresnik. Thirty-six new DH-9A bombers and sixty fresh pilots had arrived early in the summer and these were used to harass Bolshevik gunboats and troop concentrations. The day before the offensive began, a DH-9A caught a squad of enemy soldiers in the open and, as recorded by Ira Jones, "Many a Bolo was giving his dying kick as we left the battle-scarred scene, after having used up my five hundred rounds of ammunition." On 11 August seven of the airplanes started for a Bolshevik village on the Dvina when they ran into a heavy fog and only two were able to get back to Beresnik. But by the afternoon of 14 August the weather cleared sufficiently to permit a bombing attack on Puchega. Jones's aircraft dropped six phosphorous bombs from a height of 300 feet and "had a great time doing it. We could see people running all over the place and I peppered them very plentifully with my machine-gun. Three of our bombs hit houses and set them on fire. Very exciting."[13]

The only sour note was the uninspiring performance, which Ironside had predicted, of the Russians. On one occasion two companies of Russians, who were left as an occupation force at a village on the Dvina, flatly disobeyed orders and fled to the rear. Afterwards one disgusted British officer described the Russian troops as being of "very little use" and as "not worth ten British soldiers." On the railroad front, however, the Russians performed somewhat better. At the end of August, General Miller undertook a limited offensive that captured nearly 1,000 prisoners and that, as Ironside recollected, "succeeded beyond anything I had expected." In part the success was attributable to a surprise bayonet attack by two companies of Australians--members of Sadleir-Jackson's Brigade--that preceded the Russian advance.[14] Moreover, the Russian offensive on the railroad front was greatly assisted by another surprise tactic--aerial gas attacks carried out over a seven-day period by R.A.F. DH-9s.

In all, 361 bombs containing "Q" chemical were dropped on three targets on the railroad and all except three functioned well, producing a dense cloud of lethal smoke. After the initial attack at Emtsa, 120 miles to the south of Archangel, the pilots reported a "marked absence of Machine Gun and A.A. fire, the accuracy of which had previously caused trouble to our low-flying planes." One gassed prisoner testified that the very appearance of Allied planes, even if they did not actually drop gas bombs, invariably produced a mass panic among the Bolshevik soldiers. Undoubtedly the aerial gas attacks gave the Allies an important psychological advantage. Overall, Ironside was greatly pleased with the results of the August offensives and concluded that the disengaging blow "was just what we needed for our peaceful evacuation."[15]

A welcome rise in the river during the last week of August was the signal to start the withdrawal. Several deep draft gunboats were sent down river and feverish efforts were begun to lighten the five monitors by removing their ammunition, stores, and most of their fuel. In the case of the two largest monitors (M25 and M27) extreme measures were required. Both main engines and a 7.5-inch gun were removed from M25, and M27 lost all its engines and guns as well as much of its armor plating which was burned off with acetylene torches. In spite of these efforts M25 still drew six feet, two inches, and M27 drew six

feet, five inches, which was too deep to pass over
the sand bars above Beresnik. Through the use of
depth charges a channel was blasted through the upper
and lower bars at Konetzgori that enabled M25 to be
pulled across, but M27 stuck fast on the lower bar
and could not be freed. A similar fate befell M25
on the next major sand bar at Chamova.

Another project that preceded the evacuation
was the laying of an extensive mine field between
Puchega and Seltso. As a result the Bolshevik fleet
had to contend with an advanced mine field of eight
"horned" mines and a second field of fifteen "whisker"
mines. As Captain Altham explained, "These were
solely intended to delay the Enemy Flotilla and
prevent their bombarding our positions during the
evacuation." As planned, the first two mine fields
delayed the Bolsheviks for three days during which
they lost a paddle-wheel steamer that sank after
striking a mine. Once past the initial barrier the
Bolshevik flotilla had to face a third mine field
of thirty "M" sinker mines laid at Seltso in three
lines of ten each, and a final field of thirty "H"
mines laid in five rows of six each. In addition,
an extensive mine field of thirty mines was laid in
the Vaga near its junction with the Dvina. The only
hitch in the preparations was the dismal showing of
the North Russian troops. On 29 August, Sadleir-
Jackson had to disarm two companies of the 4th
North Russian Rifles as they were reported by their
commander to be on the verge of mutiny. Two days
later General Miller appeared and, while trying
to decide which of several defensive positions to
occupy, requested (to the horror of their officers)
that the two companies be rearmed. As Captain Altham
reported, "This vacillating policy, the knowledge that
at best the morale of the Russians was exceedingly
low, even where they were not actually treacherous,
their lack of organization and supplies, the very
bad quality of their officers and general instability
could not but add considerably to the difficulties of
our evacuation."[16]

Meanwhile at Archangel the last of the foreign
diplomats were packing to leave. Somewhat ironically
the task of dismantling the United States embassy, as
the old consulate was called, fell upon Felix Cole,
who had outspokenly opposed the Allied intervention
from the very beginning. Since the departure of
DeWitt Poole in mid-June, Cole had been chargé
d'affaires. Not much was left for Cole to dispose
of as the embassy's inventory was now limited to just
"one good desk, two new small Hall Marvin combination
lock safes, nine plain pine tables, 34 miscellaneous

chairs, four desk lamps, three small rugs and a
quantity of small articles of slight value."
Considering that it would cost more to ship the goods
than they were worth, Cole recommended, and the State
Department concurred, that everything should be sold
for whatever it would bring prior to the evacuation.[17]

Personal matters also intruded. Cole was faced
with the ever-present expense of maintaining his wife
and infant daughter at Harbin, Manchuria, where they
had taken refuge two years previously. Furthermore,
his wife's plan to come to Archangel in August 1919
was thwarted by Bolshevik gains in Siberia. Cole also
had to contend with a violent personality clash with
consul Shelby Strother, who wrote critical letters to
the State Department accusing Cole of having expelled
him unjustly from the embassy living quarters without
cooking utensils, and with having issued passports
to three Russian women who harbored "Bolshevik
tendencies." Cole counter-attacked by pointing out
to the State Department that Strother had refused
to move from Cole's quarters "as I had indicated he
could do without regret on my part during several of
our disputes," and had secretly offered to pay double
rent to the landlord if he would evict Cole. The
personal frictions were finally resolved by the
evacuation of the embassy on 14 September, Strother
being assigned to Amsterdam and Cole returning to
Washington. Three days later the French diplomatic
mission also left Archangel.[18]

Simultaneously the British withdrawal on the Dvina
got under way. First of all two demolition parties
blew up the bridges spanning the river roads on either
side of the Dvina. Next they dynamited the wreck of
the gunboat H.M.S. Sword Dance that had been sunk near
Tulgas by a mine on 24 June. The crews then turned
their attention to M25 and M27 that had been wired
with thirteen depth charges apiece. Short circuits
caused by rain temporarily delayed the effort. But
eventually two-thirds of the charges placed on M27
fired and, as recounted by Captain Altham, "the
ship was cut completely in two just abaft the gun
platform, the starboard side blown out, and a raging
fire was burning fore and aft before she was finally
abandoned." M25 was then blown up on Chamova bar and
"completely disintegrated, only three large but quite
unrecognisable sections and innumerable fragments
remaining."

At dawn on 16 September the British troops began
their withdrawal from the defenses at Pless. No
sooner had the evacuation begun than Sadleir-Jackson,
to his great irritation, received a telegram from
the Russian command begging him to remain until the

Russians could arrive. In the opinion of Captain
Altham: "It was obviously a Political move to throw
the responsibility for the front not being taken
over on to our shoulders. The Russian Headquarters
were at Emetskoe (80 miles behind). How completely
unjustified such delay would have been is shown by
subsequent events." What Altham referred to was the
Bolshevik ambush of the Dvina convoy at the mouth of
the Vaga, which Altham blamed entirely on the Russians
who were supposed to have secured the area. The
lead boat carrying Sadleir-Jackson was fired on by
Bolshevik machine guns and before the rest of the
convoy could be alerted a transport loaded with
troops was taken by surprise and suffered fourteen
casualties. Captain Altham soon returned the fire
with assorted Lewis guns, rifles, and a three-inch
gun that had been salvaged from M27. Finally a
marine detachment launched "a most spirited and
plucky attack" which scattered the Bolshevik machine
gunners and enabled the convoy to proceed on its way
northward. Bad weather at Beresnik cost a delay of
one day, and two more days were lost when several of
the ships grounded on a sand bar, an incident that
Altham blamed on Russian river pilots. Finally, on
the afternoon of 22 September the convoy arrived at
Archangel, leaving three monitors as a rear guard to
protect the approaches to the city by rail and by
river.[19]
     To the great relief of Rawlinson and Ironside
the atmosphere in Archangel itself remained relatively
calm, considering that it was obvious the Allies were
about to leave for good. Thus the generals' worst
fears of having to conduct a military evacuation
in an atmosphere of chaos never materialized and
Rawlinson discarded the idea of declaring himself
a military dictator. One of Rawlinson's few drastic
actions, one that horrified General Miller, was to
order the destruction of surplus ammunition and
military equipment. Like Ironside, Rawlinson
believed that the White cause was doomed and he
concluded that leaving the military stores would
guarantee that sooner or later they would be seized
by the Bolsheviks. A final drastic measure on the
part of the British was the taking of Bolshevik
hostages. Actually this policy did not originate
with Rawlinson or Ironside but with the War Office.
On 5 August Ironside was instructed: "In order
that they may be used for exchange one hundred of
the most influencial Bolshevik prisoners should be
brought to the United Kingdom and in the meantime
held as hostages for the proper treatment of British
prisoners in Russia." Subsequent negotiations with

the Bolsheviks for the exchange of prisoners failed
when the Bolsheviks demanded as a precondition that
they be permitted to send diplomatic representatives
abroad. Since this would have constituted de facto
recognition of the Bolsheviks it was rejected. As a
result forty-seven hostages were shipped to Britain
on the Kildonan Castle which sailed on 3 September,
and another fifty-four hostages went three weeks
later on the Toloa. Also departing during the same
period were 5,552 Russians who took advantage of
the opportunity to go into exile rather than face
the Bolsheviks. By 27 September the Archangel
intervention ended, slightly more than a year after
it had begun, as the last British troops boarded
transports and the three monitors were withdrawn from
their defensive positions. Last to depart was Captain
Altham, who recorded: "No hostile action took place
during the final stages of the evacuation which
proceeded in perfect order."[20]

For several months the shaky North Russian
government under Miller managed to stagger along
while the Bolsheviks concentrated upon defeating
the White Russian forces in Siberia and the South.
Temporarily the Bolsheviks refrained from launching
a winter offensive. But the defeat and execution of
Admiral Kolchak in early 1920 meant the inevitable.
By early February the remaining defenses of the North
Russians collapsed as a result of mass desertions on
the railroad and the Dvina. On 19 February General
Miller and his government fled by icebreaker to
Britain and two days later, without firing a shot,
the Bolshevik 154th Infantry Regiment entered
Archangel to receive the traditional peace offering
of bread and salt.[21]

So far as the American participants were
concerned, the North Russian expedition was by then
no more than ancient history. In mid-July the 339th
Infantry arrived at Detroit and was given a tumultuous
welcome that included a ticker tape parade and a
Chamber of Commerce reception. Within a week the
soldiers were discharged to return to their homes
and the routine of civilian life, occasionally to
reminisce about their experiences at reunions of the
Detroit-based Polar Bear Association. Like the rest
of the country, most of the soldiers wanted merely
to forget the whole unpleasant experience as soon as
possible. Many felt a sense of chagrin and rejection
for having been associated with a "mutinous" regiment
that fought an unpopular and unsuccessful war.
"Whether willfully or unwillingly," wrote John Cudahy,
"our country had engaged in an unprovoked intensive,
inglorious, little armed conflict which had ended in

disaster and disgrace." In his view the North Russian
expedition "will always remain a depraved one with
status of a free-booter's excursion."[22]

Was there nothing at all beneficial to come out
of the experience? Several of the soldiers suggested
that the nine months in Russia had turned them into
something resembling superpatriots and had made them
appreciate many things in America they had previously
taken for granted. Writing to Professor Carl Russell
Fish, Lieutenant John A. Commons remarked that
the war had "made damn good Americans out of our
soldiers. . . . And, if you should care for a very
exciting five minutes at any time, just mention
Bolshevik or I.W.W. to a member of the 339th." Or,
as expressed by Captain Robert P. Boyd, all those
lucky enough to come back from Russia alive were
certain to be "better men and better citizens, to be
more contented with less envy, willing to work and
to clean up the backyard." Certainly the Americans
had no reason to hang their heads. It was true, of
course, that the 339th Infantry was not well prepared
for its assignment. But it was also true that the
British commanders were utterly unrealistic in their
expectations. In the opinion of General Richardson,
the British seemed to think the Americans "were
imbued with some quality of inherent ferocity and
desire for blood which would cause them to do all the
fighting willingly and eagerly, even though commanded
by incompetent British officers." Based on his four
months at Archangel, Richardson concluded that the
American troops had ranked "well at the top of all
of the troops in North Russia, both as to character
and accomplishment." Transported by an historical
accident from the pastoral life of Michigan and
Wisconsin to the tragicomedy of the Archangel
intervention, the soldiers of the 339th Infantry were
deserving of the eulogistic sentiments expressed by
Senator Hiram Johnson: "They served under conditions
that were the most confusing and perplexing that an
American army was ever asked to contend with, but
they did their duty."[23]

In Britain as in America there was no inclination
to indulge in a lengthy and painful postmortem. A
general consensus was reached in government circles
that Britain had made an effort in North Russia that
was beyond the call of duty and that through no fault
of her own Britain had reached the end of the road.
As expressed by General Wilson: "The position had to
be faced that the British Empire in common with all
the Entente nations, was weary and exhausted, depleted
in men and money, and incapable of further military
efforts on a grand scale." Thus the time had come to

recognize that "North Russia offered no prospects of
decisive results, and with Kolchak's failure any
sustained military effort in that theatre was doomed
to be barren." None of the planners and supporters
of the affair rushed to shoulder responsibility for
the failure of the Anglo-American expedition, but
conveniently placed the blame on the blundering White
Russian generals and politicians. In this regard,
Wilson approvingly quoted Captain Altham's statement,
"The instability of the Russian troops, the lack of
discipline, organizing ability and military leadership
of the Russian officers and Higher Command after a
year of the most loyal and capable British support,
soon made it evident that to continue that support
would be fruitless."[24]

In his final report on naval operations Captain
Altham expressed the hope that "the very gallant work
performed by the officers and men who bore the brunt
of the fighting in this distant and little known
part of the world may not be forgotten." But in the
West just the opposite was true as memories of the
Archangel expedition were quick to fade. However,
this was not so much the case in the Soviet Union
where the political, as opposed to the military, side
of the subject was kept alive in the form of distorted
official histories marred by ideological bias, lack
of objectivity, and uncritical assumptions concerning
the conspiratorial designs of "aggressive imperialist
circles." Initially Soviet historians of the
intervention treated the United States rather
leniently with Britain and France being depicted
as the primary villains. Not until the Cold War
did the United States emerge as the main instigator.
Representative of the legacy of distrust arising from
the Allied involvement was Premier Nikita Khrushchev's
remark made in 1959: "We remember the grim days when
American soldiers went to our soil headed by their
generals. . . . Never have any of our soldiers been
on American soil, but your soldiers were on Russian
soil. These are the facts."[25]

That the weak Anglo-American intervention was,
as Bruce Lockhart wrote, "a blunder comparable
with the worst mistakes of the Crimean War" is
undeniable.[26] And, as in the case of the Crimean
conflict, the pertinent military lessons were all
but ignored by both sides. As a result, and to
their sorrow, Soviet generals in the Russo-Finnish
Winter War of 1939-1940 and German generals during
the Russian campaign of World War II were forced to
relearn that in winter a well-organized and sheltered
defense enjoys a significant advantage over the
offense, that motorized vehicles are often inoperable

and often inferior to the Siberian pony, that
weapons of all kinds are likely to freeze at subzero
temperatures, that well-trained and acclimatized
troops provided with the warmest equipment are
absolutely essential, and that even minor injuries
can be fatal unless immediate shelter and medical
care are made available. Apparently the small scale
of the fighting, its indecisive character, and the
fairly modest loss of life explain why both sides
learned little from their combat experiences under
arctic conditions. Only 222 Americans and 317
Englishmen lost their lives in North Russia. Russian
losses--both White and Bolshevik--are unknown, but
were certainly far greater than those of the Allies.
Still, the casualties seemed inconsequential when
compared with the bloody campaigns on the eastern
and western fronts.

In the opinion of General Henry Wilson, one
lesson stood out above all others: "It is that,
once a military force is involved in operations on
land it is almost impossible to limit the magnitude
of its commitments." From the landing of 150 British
marines at Murmansk in April 1918, the force swelled
by bits and pieces until more than 18,000 British
troops were involved a year later. In view of the
unhappy British experience in North Russia, the chief
of the Imperial General Staff urged that future
requests for "even a company or two" of troops
should not be agreed to "without the fullest and
most careful consideration of the larger obligations
which such compliance may ultimately involve." Surely
the Western powers would have saved themselves much
embarrassment had they listened to the advice of Felix
Cole: "Intervention will begin on a small scale
but with each step forward will grow in its demands
for ships, men, money, and materials. . . . If we
intervene, going farther into Russia as we succeed, we
shall be swallowed up."[27] By ignoring Cole's counsel
the Allies, as Cole himself suggested, may well have
sold their birthright in Russia for a mess of pottage.

Notes

Works frequently cited have been identified by the following abbreviations:

DSNA General Records of the Department of State, National Archives

FRUS Papers relating to the Foreign Relations of the United States, 1918: Russia

MHC Michigan Historical Collections

PRO Public Record Office

PWW The Papers of Woodrow Wilson

SHSW State Historical Society of Wisconsin

Chapter 1.

1. Malcolm K. Whyte, a member of the 310th Engineers, wrote to his wife, "You will not hear from me for a long time perhaps months due to a long trip that we are about to start on. I will not be able to mention the place in my letter. . . . The gaps in mail this winter will likewise be long. Don't worry if you do not hear from me for months." Malcolm K. Whyte to his wife, 24 August 1918, William F. Whyte Papers, State Historical Society of Wisconsin, hereafter cited as SHSW. Henry Dennis to his father, Madison Democrat, 22 December 1918, Wisconsin War History Commission, Clipping File, 1916-1919, SHSW; Robert P. Boyd to his parents, Eau Claire Leader, 7 January 1919, Wisconsin War History Commission, Clipping File, 1916-1919, SHSW.

2. W. C. Butts to his parents, Milwaukee
Sentinel, 10 March 1919, Wisconsin War History
Commission, Clipping File, 1916-1919, SHSW.
3. The standard work, written by an anti-
Bolshevik Russian emigre, is Leonid I.
Strakhovsky, Intervention at Archangel: The Story of Allied
Intervention and Russian Counter-Revolution in North
Russia, 1918-1920 (Princeton, 1944). Strakhovsky's
study has now been superseded by George F.
Kennan, Soviet-American Relations, 1917-1920, vol. 1, Russia
Leaves the War (Princeton, 1956); and vol. 2, The
Decision to Intervene (Princeton, 1958); and Richard
H. Ullman, Anglo-Soviet Relations, 1917-1921, vol. 1,
Intervention and the War (Princeton, 1961); and
vol. 2, Britain and the Russian Civil War (Princeton,
1968). Other scholarly studies that touch upon the
North Russian intervention are John Bradley, Allied
Intervention in Russia (London, 1968); John Bradley,
Civil War in Russia, 1917-1920 (London, 1975);
N. Gordon Levin, Jr., Woodrow Wilson and World
Politics: America's Response to War and Revolution
(New York, 1968); John M. Thompson, Russia,
Bolshevism, and the Versailles Peace (Princeton,
1966); Betty Miller Unterberger, America's Siberian
Expedition, 1918-1920: A Study of National Policy
(Durham, 1956); and Betty Miller Unterberger, ed.,
American Intervention in the Russian Civil War
(Lexington, Mass., 1969). The North Russian
expedition has been the subject of several
journalistic accounts: E. M. Halliday, The Ignorant
Armies: The Anglo-American Archangel Expedition,
1918-1919 (London, 1958); David Footman, Civil War in
Russia (London, 1961), pp. 184-206; Richard Goldhurst,
The Midnight War: The American Intervention in
Russia, 1918-1920 (New York, 1978), pp. 85-115,
135-48; Robert Jackson, At War with the Bolsheviks:
The Allied Intervention into Russia, 1917-1920
(London, 1972), pp. 32-42, 67-88, 151-72; John
Silverlight, The Victor's Dilemma: Allied
Intervention in the Russian Civil War (London, 1970),
pp. 57-60, 74-77, 172-98, 246-57; and John Swettenham,
Allied Intervention in Russia, 1918-1919 (London,
1967), pp. 187-200. Several participants have
published books detailing their experiences: Joel R.
Moore, Harry H. Mead, and Lewis E. Jahns, The History
of the American Expedition Fighting the Bolsheviki:
Campaigning in North Russia, 1918-1919 (Detroit,
1920); John Cudahy [A Chronicler], Archangel: The
American War with Russia (Chicago, 1924); David R.
Francis, Russia from the American Embassy (New York,
1921); and Sir Edmund Ironside, Archangel 1918-1919
(London, 1953). Soviet "scholarly" literature on the

Allied intervention, as John M. Thompson points out
in "Allied and American Intervention in Russia,
1918-1921," in Rewriting Russian History: Soviet
Interpretations of Russia's Past, ed. Cyril E. Black
(New York, 1956), pp. 334-400; is badly marred by
ideological bias, lack of objectivity, and uncritical
assumptions concerning the sinister designs of
"world imperialism." George F. Kennan, "Soviet
Historiography and America's Role in the
Intervention," American Historical Review 65 (January
1960):302-22, finds recent Soviet historiography
concerning the Allied intervention to be seriously
defective due to its systematic misuse of evidence
and its reliance on such cliches as "American
imperialists," "American reactionaries," "American
capitalists," "imperialist circles of the U.S.A.,"
"American bourgeois politicians," "the
interventionists," "aggressive imperialist circles,"
"American millionaires," and "American leading
circles." Anatole Mazour, The Writing of History in
the Soviet Union (Palo Alto, 1971), pp. 249-52; also
stresses the amateurish quality of Soviet history.
Soviet historians N. V. Sivachev and N. N. Yakovlev,
Russia and the United States (Chicago, 1979), pp.
42-62; emphasize the "counterrevolutionary essence"
of the American intervention. The most recent
scholarship on the subject is contained in Eugene
Trani, "Woodrow Wilson and the Decision to Intervene
in Russia: A Reconsideration," Journal of Modern
History 48 (September, 1976):440-61, and John W. Long,
"American Intervention in Russia: The North Russian
Expedition, 1918-1919," Diplomatic History 6 (Winter,
1982):45-67. Trani plausibly suggests that President
Wilson succumbed to Allied pressure for intervention.
The primary consideration influencing the president
was a feeling that America as a member of a war
coalition must cooperate with its allies. But
at the same time, the president was so harassed by
the demands of domestic politics, mobilization, war
strategy, and peacemaking, that he was unable to give
much serious thought to the Russian situation. The
latter essay by Long demonstrates that "there is
simply no evidence to support the contention that
President Wilson was motivated by an ideological
desire to crush Bolshevism and convert the Russians
to his own political convictions" (67). Long's essay
contains an excellent survey of current Soviet
historiography concerning the Allied intervention
in North Russia.

    4. Long, "American Intervention," p. 54; March
to Baker, 24 June 1918, Arthur S. Link et al., eds.,
The Papers of Woodrow Wilson, 55 vols. to date

(Princeton, 1966-), 48:418-21 (hereafter cited as
PWW); Peyton C. March, The Nation at War (Garden
City, 1932), p. 113; Trani, "Wilson and the Decision
to Intervene," pp. 447-50; Unterberger, America's
Siberian Expedition, pp. 63-64.

5. Kennan, Decision to Intervene, pp. 44-57;
W. B. Fowler, British-American Relations, 1917-1918:
The Role of Sir William Wiseman (Princeton, 1969),
pp. 164-97; Wilson to Secretary of the Navy Josephus
Daniels, 8 April 1918, PWW 47:290.

6. Fowler, British-American Relations, pp.
138-53; Ullman, Intervention and the War, pp. 172-73.

7. Henry P. Beers, U.S. Naval Forces in Northern
Russia (Archangel and Murmansk), 1918-1919
(Washington, 1943), pp. 7-8; Ullman, Intervention and
the War, pp. 178-79.

8. Ullman, Intervention and the War, pp. 186-95;
Kennan, Decision to Intervene, pp. 268-69; Balfour
to Lansing, 28 May 1918, Department of State, Papers
Relating to the Foreign Relations of the United
States, 1918: Russia, 3 vols. (Washington,
1931-1932), pp. 2, 476 (hereafter cited as FRUS);
Balfour to Reading, 29 May 1918, enclosed in Lansing
to Wilson, 31 May 1918, PWW 38:206-8.

9. Ullman, Intervention and the War, pp. 195-96;
Balfour to Reading, 11 June 1918, PWW 48:284-88.

10. Jamie H. Cockfield, ed., Dollars and
Diplomacy: Ambassador David Rowland Francis and the
Fall of Tsarism, 1916-1917 (Durham, 1981), pp. 4-7;
Gilbert C. Kohlenberg, "David Rowland Francis:
American Businessman in Russia," Mid-America 29
(October, 1958): 195-217. The ambassador's 1916
income tax return, dated 27 February 1917, is in the
David R. Francis Papers, Box 24, Missouri Historical
Society, St. Louis, Missouri.

11. Philip Jordan to William H. Lee, 18 January
1918, Mrs. Clinton A. Bliss, "Philip Jordan's Letters
from Russia, 1917-1919," Missouri Historical Society
Bulletin (January, 1958), pp. 153-54; Kennan, Russia
Leaves the War, p. 440.

12. Francis, Russia from the American Embassy,
p. 5; William Appleman Williams, American-Russian
Relations, 1781-1947 (New York, 1952), pp. 113-14;
Francis to Perry Francis, 25 September 1917, Francis
Papers, Box 27; Francis to Perry Francis, 26 November
1917, Francis Papers, Box 28; Francis to Perry
Francis, 23 April 1918, Francis Papers, Box 33.

13. Kennan, Decision to Intervene, pp. 115-35;
Francis to Maddin Summers, 14 April 1918, Francis
Papers, Box 33.

14. Kennan, Decision to Intervene, pp. 211-12;
Francis to Lansing, 13 April 1918, FRUS, 1918:

Russia, 2:124; Francis to Lansing, 2 May 1918,
FRUS, 1918: Russia, 1:519-21.

    15. Russia: Coast Report, August, 1918, Naval
Records Collection of the Office of Naval Records and
Library, Box 605, RG 45 (National Archives); J. N.
Westwood, A History of Russian Railways (London,
1964), pp. 172-73; Jacqueline St. John, "John F.
Stevens: American Assistance to Russian and Siberian
Railroads, 1917-1922" (Ph.D. dissertation, University
of Oklahoma, 1969), p. 23; Kennan, Decision to
Intervene, p. 17.

    16. Cole to Lansing, 6 January 1918, RG 59,
General Records of the Department of State, File No.
861.00/1715, National Archives (hereafter cited as
DSNA).

    17. Cole to Lansing, 28 January 1918, RG 59,
861.00/1719, DSNA; Francis to Lansing, 22 July 1918,
FRUS, 1918: Russia, 2:502-3.

    18. Cole to Lansing, 8 February 1918, RG 59,
861.00/1720, DSNA. Subsequently, the naval
commander-in-chief, Eugene Somoff, was reinstated,
but was stripped of all but "a small fraction of the
power wielded by him six months ago" (Cole to Lansing,
16 February 1918, RG 59, 861.00/1721, DSNA); Kennan,
Decision to Intervene, pp. 16-21; Ullman, Intervention
and the War, p. 113.

    19. University of Wisconsin, Directory of Offices
and Students (Madison, 1905), p. 35; Harvard College
Class of 1910, Twenty-Fifth Anniversary Report
(Cambridge, 1935), pp. 139-40; Department of State,
Register of the Department of State (Washington,
1930); Cole to Lansing, 1 April 1918, RG 59,
123C673/14, DSNA.

    20. William C. Huntington to David R. Francis,
26 May 1917, Francis Papers, Box 26.

    21. Memorandum by the Acting Chief of the
Archangel Fleet Counter Intelligence Bureau, A. Tam,
1 December 1917, RG 84, Records of the Foreign
Service Posts of the Department of State, 12F54, DSNA.

    22. Cole to consul Roger Culver Tredwell,
25 September 1917, RG 84, 12F54, DSNA.

    23. Memorandum by A. Tam, 1 December 1917, RG 84,
12F54, DSNA.

    24. Cole to Lansing, 15 January 1918, RG 59,
125.1462/1; Wilbur J. Carr, Director of the Consular
Service, to Cole, 11 May 1917, RG 59, 125.1462/7a,
DSNA.

    25. Marine Note of Protest Ledger, October 1917,
RG 84, 12F54, DSNA; Major C. T. Williams, Deputy
Commissioner American Red Cross to Cole, 3 December
1918, RG 84, 12F54, DSNA.

26. Cole to Francis, 26 January 1918, RG 59, 861.00/1719, DSNA.

27. Francis to Lansing, 23 March 1918, FRUS, 1918: Russia, 3:111-12; Lansing to Francis, 27 March 1918, ibid., p. 113; Francis to Lansing, 20 April 1918, ibid., p. 119; Francis to Lansing, 23 March 1918, ibid., p. 111.

28. Cole to Francis, 1 June 1918, FRUS, 1918: Russia, 2:477-84.

29. Cole to Francis, 14 June 1918, RG 84, 12F54, DSNA; Cole to Francis, 19 June 1918, RG 84, 12F54, DSNA.

30. Francis to Cole, 13 June 1918, Francis Papers, Box 33; Cole to Francis, 2 July 1918, ibid., Box 34; Francis to Cole, 21 July 1918, ibid.

31. Poole to Francis, 6 July 1918 (memorandums from Poole to F. Willoughby Smith, 25 June 1918, and Smith to Poole, 3 July 1918 enclosed), Francis Papers, Box 34.

32. Trani, "Wilson and the Decision to Intervene," p. 458; Kennan, Decision to Intervene, p. 367 f.n.

33. March, The Nation at War, pp. 124-25; Unterberger, America's Siberian Expedition, pp. 69-70.

34. Trani, "Wilson and the Decision to Intervene," p. 459; Excerpt from the diary of Josephus Daniels, 9 July 1918, PWW 48:578; Lansing to the Allied ambassadors, 17 July 1918, FRUS, 1918: Russia, 2:287-90; Cole to Francis, 1 June 1918, ibid., p. 478.

Chapter 2.

1. Edward Altham, "The Dwina Campaign," Journal of the Royal United Service Institution 68 (February, 1923):231-32; Henry Newbolt, History of the Great War Based on Official Documents, Naval Operations, vol. 5 (London, 1931), pp. 322-23; J. J. Colledge, Ships of the Royal Navy: An Historical Index, vol. 1, (Devon, England, 1969), pp. 57, 376.

2. Francis, Russia from the American Embassy, p. 266.

3. Cole to Lansing, 22 July 1918, FRUS, 1918: Russia, 2:499-502; Footman, Civil War in Russia, p. 179.

4. Francis, Russia from the American Embassy, p. 261; Kennan, Decision to Intervene, pp. 422-25, 450-52.

5. Poole to the War Office, 5 October 1918, WO158/714/HMO6495, Public Record Office (hereafter cited as PRO); Strakhovsky, Intervention at Archangel, p. 15.

6. Altham, "The Dwina Campaign," pp. 232-33;
Ira Jones, An Air-Fighter's Scrap-Book (London,
1938), pp. 120-21; Memorandum by Captain Bierer,
3 August 1918, Strakhovsky, Intervention at Archangel,
Appendix I, pp. 261-64.

7. J. I. Starbuck, "The R.A.F. in Russia," The
Aeroplane, 17 (July, 1919):82; S. F. Wise, Canadian
Airmen and the First World War (Toronto, 1980),
p. 624; Roy MacLaren, Canadians in Russia, 1918-1919
(Toronto, 1976), p. 65; Poole to the War Office,
5 October 1918, WO158/714/HMO6495, PRO.

8. Strakhovsky, Intervention at Archangel,
p. 18; Poole to the War Office, 5 October 1918,
WO158/714/HMO6495, PRO.

9. Cole to Lansing, 6 August 1918, FRUS, 1918:
Russia, 2:509-12.

10. Strakhovsky, Intervention at Archangel,
pp. 21-28; Memorandum by Captain Bierer, 3 August
1918, ibid., Appendix I, pp. 261-64; Cole to Lansing,
10 September 1918, FRUS, 1918: Russia, 2:527-30.

11. Altham, "The Dwina Campaign," p. 233; Poole
to the War Office, 4 August 1918, WO106/1153/HMO6606,
PRO; Jones, An Air-Fighter's Scrap-Book, p. 122;
Memorandum by Finlayson, 16 March 1919,
WO158/714/HMO6495, PRO; Francis to William H. Lee,
4 September 1918, Francis Papers, Box 34; Supreme War
Council, "Allied Intervention in Siberia and Russia,"
2 July 1918, CAB/122/HMO6737, PRO.

12. Poole to the War Office, 6 August 1918,
WO106/1153/HMO6606, PRO; Kennan, Decision to
Intervene, p. 425; Dennis Gordon, Quartered in Hell:
The Story of the American North Russian Expeditionary
Force, 1918-1919 (Missoula, Montana, 1982), pp. 7,
53; Poole to the War Office, 17 August 1918,
WO158/712/HMO6477, PRO.

13. Poole to the War Office, 5 October 1918,
WO158/714/HMO6495, PRO.

14. Andrew Soutar, With Ironside in North Russia
(London, 1940), pp. 91-92; Poole to the War Office,
5 October 1918, WO158/714/HMO6495, PRO.

15. Altham, "The Dwina Campaign," p. 236;
Josselyn, "Notes on experience of river fighting in
1918," no date, WO158/711; Poole to the War Office,
5 October 1918, WO158/714/HMO6495, PRO.

16. Memorandum by Finlayson, 16 March 1919,
WO158/714/HMO6737, PRO; Poole to the War Office,
5 October 1918, WO158/714/HMO6495, PRO; Cole to
Francis, 1 June 1918, FRUS, 1918: Russia, 2:479.

17. Poole to the War Office, 5 October 1918,
WO158/714/HMO6495, PRO; Ullman, Intervention and
the War, pp. 237-43.

18. Poole to the War Office, 5 October 1918,
WO158/714/HMO6495, PRO; Cole to Lansing, 1 June 1918,
FRUS, 1918: Russia, 2:478-79.
19. Poole to the War Office, 17 August 1918,
WO158/712/HMO6477, PRO; Poole to the War Office,
9 September 1918, WO106/1155/HMO6615, PRO; Poole to
the War Office, 15 September 1918, WO158/714; Cole
to Francis, 1 June 1918, FRUS, 1918: Russia, 2:477,
480-81; Robert Hamilton Bruce Lockhart, British Agent
(London, 1933), p. 308.

Chapter 3.

1. Kennan, Decision to Intervene, p. 426; Long,
"American Intervention," p. 56.
2. Richard M. Doolen, Michigan's Polar Bears:
The American Expedition to North Russia, 1918-1919
(Ann Arbor, 1965), pp. 3-28; Gordon W. Smith, "Waging
War in 'Frozen Hell': A Record of Personal
Experiences," Current History (April, 1930), pp.
69-70; Interview with Major J. Brooks Nichols,
Detroit Free Press, 1 July 1919; Frederick Evans,
"Campaigning in Arctic Russia," Journal of the Royal
United Service Institution 66 (May, 1941):296.
3. Gordon, Quartered in Hell, p. 179; Diary of
John S. Crissman, 25 August 1918, Michigan Historical
Collections, Bentley Historical Library, University
of Michigan (hereafter cited as MHC); Diary of
Kenneth A. Skellenger, 25 August 1918, MHC; Diary
of Edwin Arkins, 2, 5 September 1918, MHC.
4. Moore, Mead, and Jahns, Fighting the
Bolsheviki, pp. 15-18; Gordon, Quartered in Hell,
p. 64; "Lieutenant Marcus T. Casey," in John G.
Gregory, "The Polar Bear Expedition," an unpublished
manuscript without page numbers, Records of the
Wisconsin War History Commission, SHSW.
5. Moore, Mead, and Jahns, Fighting the
Bolsheviki, pp. 98-99; Charles Ryan to John R.
Commons, 18 December 1918, Madison Democrat, 21 March
1919, Wisconsin War History Commission, Clipping File,
1916-1919, SHSW; American Sentinel, 25 January 1919,
ibid.
6. "Extract from Report of Chief Surgeon Jonas R.
Longley," no date, Records of the American
Expeditionary Forces, 1917-1923, Box 1548, RG 120.
7. "To Keep Fit in North Russia," undated
pamphlet, WO95/5420, PRO; Poole to Colonel George
Stewart, 25 September 1918, Historical Files of the
American Expeditionary Force, North Russia, 1918-1919,
(Washington, 1973), National Archives Microfilm
Publication M924, reel 2; Major Jonas R. Longley,

1 April 1919, "Report of the work accomplished by the Medical Department since arrival in Northern Russia," M924, reel 2; Liuetenant Colonel Edward S. Thurston to General Wilds P. Richardson, 20 June 1919, Records of the American Expeditionary Forces, 1917-1923, Box 1548, RG 120.

8. Ullman, Intervention and the War, pp. 246-48; Francis, Russia from the American Embassy, pp. 270-75; Moore, Mead, and Jahns, Fighting the Bolsheviki, pp. 39-40; Art Wickham to Michael Macalla, 20 July 1966, Papers of Michael Macalla, MHC; Footman, Civil War in Russia, pp. 182-83.

9. Poole to the War Office, 9 September 1918, WO106/1155/HMO6615, PRO.

10. Moore, Mead, and Jahns, Fighting the Bolsheviki, pp. 19-21.

11. Unsigned memorandum by officer in command of trench mortar platoon, 1 October 1918, M924, reel 2; Memorandum by Major C. G. Young, 12 October 1918, ibid.

12. Memorandum by Major J. Brooks Nichols, 23 October 1918, M924, reel 2; Poole to the War Office, 13 October 1918, WO106/1155/HMO6615, PRO; Diary of Charles B. Ryan, 17 September, 3 October 1918, MHC; Jay H. Bonnell, "Reminiscence of the Polar Bear Expedition to North Russia," no date, MHC; Ernest Reed, "The Story of the A.E.F. in North Russia," Current History (April, 1930), p. 65.

13. Arkins Diary, 8 September 1918, MHC; Henry Katz, "Short Summary of Activities of Medical Personnel With First Battalion 339th Infantry," no date, ibid.; Gordon, Quartered in Hell, pp. 207, 217.

14. Arkins Diary, 14, 19 September 1918, MHC.

15. Jackson, At War with the Bolsheviks, pp. 69-74; Newbolt, Naval Operations, pp. 330-32; Poole to the War Office, 24 September 1918, WO106/1155/HMO6495, PRO.

16. Poole to the War Office, 5 October 1918, WO158/714/HMO6495, PRO; Jackson, At War with the Bolsheviks, p. 70; Gordon, Quartered in Hell, p. 207; Diary of Henry Katz, 16 September 1918, MHC.

17. Weeks Diary, 13, 15, 21 September 1918, SHSW; Arkins Diary, 21 September 1918, MHC; Crissman Diary, 4 October 1918, MHC; Gordon, Quartered in Hell, p. 210.

18. Poole to the War Office, 29 September 1918, WO106/1153/HMO6606, PRO; Poole to the War Office, 5 October 1918, WO158/714/HMO6495, PRO.

19. Eau Claire, Wisconsin, Leader, 25 July 1919, Wisconsin War History Commission, Clipping File, 1916-1919, SHSW; Ironside, Archangel, p. 25; "You must realise that our situation here is not a bed of roses.

The large labour element in Archangel is still tainted with Bolshevism and it only needs a set back at the front to start open antagonism. . . . I am not in the least nervous of the final result, but I realise that the prospect with our present forces can only be looked on as a gamble which will, I am confident, give you a magnificent return, but even if it fails through drawing away from the Western front a considerable body of German troops I consider that our failure will have contributed to your final success in no small part," Poole to the War Office, 22 August 1918, WO106/1161/HMO6666, PRO.

20. Instructions for General Poole, 18 May 1918, WO106/1161/HMO6666, PRO; The War Office to Poole, 10 August 1918, WO106/1153/HMO6606, PRO.

21. Francis to Lansing, 27 August 1918, FRUS, 1918: Russia, 2:513-14; Francis to Lansing, 3 September 1918, ibid., pp. 517-19.

22. Bliss to March, 7 September 1918, PWW 51:52-55; Bliss to Francis, 3 October 1918, Francis Papers, Box 35.

23. Wilson to Lansing, 5 September 1918, PWW 49:48; Lansing to Wilson, 11 September 1918, PWW 49:515-17; Wilson to Lansing, 18 September 1918, PWW 51:50-51.

24. Wilson to Lansing, 26 September 1918, PWW 51:121-22; Lansing to Francis, 26 September 1918, FRUS, 1918: Russia, 2:546.

25. Poole to the War Office, 13 October 1918, WO106/1155/HMO6615, PRO.

26. Statement of General Tasker Bliss to the Supreme War Council, 6 October 1918, CAB125/123/HMO6721, PRO; Ironside, Archangel, p. 13; The War Office to General Officer in Command at Archangel, 16 October 1919, WO106/1153/HMO6606, PRO; The War Office to Ironside, 11 November 1918, WO158/712/HMO6477, PRO; Ironside to the War Office, 6 November 1918, WO158/714/HMO6495, PRO.

Chapter 4.

1. Ironside, Archangel, pp. 11-13; Swettenham, Allied Intervention in Russia, p. 53; Ironside to the War Office, 12 June 1919, WO106/1164/HMO6679, PRO.

2. Richard Carroll, "The Polar Bear Army," Liberty Magazine (7 September, 1929), pp. 33-37; Stewart to Colonel Richard Dupuy, 5 November 1940, Papers of Colonel George Evans Stewart, United States Military Academy Library, Special Collections Division.

3. Francis, Russia from the American Embassy, p. 295; Cudahy, Archangel, pp. 68-69; Ironside,

Archangel, pp. 37-38; Cole to Francis, 1 June 1918, FRUS, 1918: Russia, 2:480.

4. Ironside, Archangel, p. 43.

5. "Final Consolidated Report of the 310th Engineers, Archangel, Russia," 20 June 1919, William F. Whyte Papers, SHSW; General Wilds P. Richardson, Notes on the War and on the North Russian Expedition, no date, M924, reel 2; Norman Shrive, ed., Frank J. Shrive, The Diary of a P.B.O.* Poor Bloody Observer (Erin, Ontario, 1981), 27 March 1919, p. 79.

6. Swettenham, Allied Intervention in Russia, pp. 75-76; Ralph Albertson, Fighting Without a War: An Account of Military Intervention in North Russia (New York, 1920), pp. 18-19; Crissman Diary, 4 October 1918, MHC; Diary of Henry Katz, 26 September 1918, MHC; Weeks Diary, 5, 6, 11, 13, 18, 20, 28 October 1918, SHSW.

7. Gordon, Quartered in Hell, pp. 86-87; Moore, Mead, and Jahns, Fighting the Bolsheviki, p. 244; Arkins Diary, 24 September 1918, MHC; Memoir of Kenneth A. Skellenger, no date, MHC.

8. Group Captain G. E. Livock, To the Ends of the Air (London, 1973), p. 65; Gordon, Quartered in Hell, pp. 196, 222; Bliss, "Philip Jordan's Letters," pp. 161-62.

9. Gordon, Quartered in Hell, p. 86; Livock, To the Ends of the Air, p. 64; "The Creation of Russia," an anonymous poem enclosed in Weeks Diary, SHSW; the poem is also printed (pp. 301-2) in Gordon, Quartered in Hell, a work which takes its name from the poem; the "Creation of Russia" is also found verbatim in Jones, An Air-Fighter's Scrap-Book, pp. 156-57, with the exception that his version reads "The average British Tommy/would sooner be quartered in Hell;" Moore, Mead and Jahns, Fighting the Bolsheviki, pp. 164-65.

10. Gordon, Quartered in Hell, p. 44; Joel R. Moore, "M" Company, 339th Infantry in North Russia (Jackson, Michigan, 1920), no page numbers; Livock, To the Ends of the Air, p. 65.

11. Moore, Mead, and Jahns, Fighting the Bolsheviki, p. 179; Gordon, Quartered in Hell, p. 181; B. F. Broaddus, "Polar Bear Materials," MHC.

12. MacLaren, Canadians in Russia, p. 65; S. F. Wise, Canadian Airmen, pp. 623-26, 627-28; Air Ministry, Synopsis of British Air-Effort During the War (London, 1919), p. 14.

13. First Lieutenant E. O. Munn to Colonel J. A. Ruggles, 16 April 1919, Records of the American Expeditionary Forces, 1917-1923, Box 268, RG 120, National Archives.

14. Grey to Ironside, 13 June 1919,
WO106/1164/HMO6679, PRO.
15. Starbuck, "The R.A.F. in Russia," pp. 85-86.
16. Shrive, Diary of a P.B.O., 31 October, 3, 13,
17, 19 November 1918, pp. 61-62, 64-67.
17. Ibid., 11 November 1918, p. 63.
18. Ibid., 16 November 1918, p. 65.

Chapter 5.

1. Memorandum by Finlayson, 16 March 1919,
WO158/714/HMO6495, PRO; Ironside, Archangel, p. 21;
Ironside to the War Office, 8 November 1918,
WO158/714/HMO6495, PRO; Cudahy, Archangel, p. 178.
2. Finlayson to Ironside, 8 October 1918,
WO158/716/HMO6512, PRO; Ironside to the War Office,
19 October 1918, WO106/1153/HMO6606, PRO;
Ironside to the War Office, 6 November 1918,
WO158/714/HMO6495, PRO.
3. Ironside to the War Office, 6 November 1918,
WO158/714/HMO6495, PRO; Ironside to the War Office,
8 November 1918, WO158/714/HMO6495, PRO.
4. Finlayson to Ironside, 1 November 1918,
WO158/714/HMO6495, PRO.
5. "Extract from General Finlayson's report,"
17 November 1918, Stewart Papers.
6. Ironside to the War Office, 6 November 1918,
WO158/714/HMO6495, PRO; Ironside to the War Office,
8 November 1918, WO158/714/HMO6495, PRO; Memorandum
by Finlayson, 16 March 1919, WO158/714/HMO6495, PRO.
7. Ironside to the War Office, 8 November 1918,
WO158/714/HMO6495, PRO; Ironside to the War Office,
6 November 1918, WO158/714/HMO6495, PRO.
8. Ironside to the War Office, 6 November 1918,
WO158/714/HMO6495, PRO; Ironside, Archangel, pp.
33-34; Ironside to the War Office, 9 January 1919,
WO158/714/HMO6495, PRO; Richardson to the Adjutant
General of the Army, 22 July 1919, Records of the
American Expeditionary Forces, 1917-1923, Box 268,
RG 120.
9. Moore, Mead, and Jahns, Fighting the
Bolsheviki, p. 179; Gordon, Quartered in Hell, p. 181.
10. Biographical sketch of Colonel George Evans
Stewart, Stewart Papers.
11. The War Department to Stewart, 28 September
1918, Stewart Papers; Ironside, Archangel, p. 34;
J. Brooks Nichols to Stewart, 8 March 1919 (marginal
notation by Stewart), Stewart Papers.
12. Bukowski to Colonel James A. Ruggles,
24 October 1918, Strakhovsky, Intervention at
Archangel, Appendix IV, pp. 274-79; Captain Eugene

Prince, "Morale of American Troops on the Dvina
Front," 2 February 1919, M924, reel 2.

   13. Memorandum by Major Jonas R. Longley,
15 March 1919, Stewart Papers; Gordon, Quartered in
Hell, pp. 171-73; Richardson to the Adjutant General
of the Army, 23 July 1919, Records of the American
Expeditionary Forces, 1917-1923, Box 268, RG 120;
Stewart to Colonel Richard Ernest Dupuy, 5 November
1940, Stewart Papers.

   14. Higgins to Stewart, 6 December 1918, Stewart
Papers; Ironside to the War Office, 12 June 1919,
WO106/1164/HMO6679, PRO; Bukowski to Ruggles,
24 October 1918, Appendix IV, Strakhovsky,
Intervention at Archangel, pp. 274-79.

   15. Ironside to the War Office, 8 November 1918,
WO158/714/HMO6495, PRO; Ironside to the War Office,
12 June 1919, WO106/1164/HMO6679, PRO.

   16. Lieutenant Colonel Ivan Ivanovitch Michaeff
to Ironside, no date, M924, reel 2; Ironside to the
War Office, 12 June 1919, WO106/1164/HMO6679, PRO;
Strakhovsky, Intervention at Archangel, pp. 101-2.

   17. Ironside to the War Office, 8 November 1918,
WO158/714/HMO6495, PRO; Ironside, Archangel, pp.
46-47; Strakhovsky, Intervention at Archangel, pp.
98, 119.

   18. Ironside, Archangel, pp. 57, 68; Ullman,
Britain and the Russian Civil War, p. 22; Ironside to
the War Office, 12 June 1919, WO106/1164/HMO6679, PRO.

   19. Ironside to the War Office, 12 June 1919,
WO106/1164/HMO6679, PRO; Albertson, Fighting Without
a War, pp. 6-7; Ironside to the War Office, 9 January
1919, WO158/714/HMO6495, PRO.

   20. Albertson, Fighting Without a War, pp. 39-44;
Richardson to the Adjutant General of the Army,
23 July 1919, Records of the American Expeditionary
Forces, 1917-1923, Box 268, RG 120.

   21. Herman F. Scheiter, Jr. to Emil Haller,
22 February 1919, contained in an undated "Charge
Sheet" detailing violations by Scheiter of censorship
regulations, Records of the American Expeditionary
Forces, 1917-1923, Box 1548, RG 120; Charles A.
Thornton to Mrs. O. M. Thornton, 23 February 1919,
enclosed in Lieutenant Colonel Edward S. Thurston
to Colonel George Stewart, 15 March 1919, Records
of the American Expeditionary Forces, 1917-1923, Box
1548, RG 120.

   22. Cudahy, Archangel, p. 70; Richardson to the
Adjutant General of the Army, July, no date, 1919,
Wilds P. Richardson Papers, United States Army
Military History Institute, Carlisle Barracks,
Pennsylvania.

23. Gordon, <u>Quartered in Hell</u>, pp. 44-45; Ironside
to the War Office, 12 June 1919, WO106/1164/HMO6679,
PRO.

Chapter 6.

1. Dvina Force, Intelligence Summary No. 1,
16 November 1918, WO157/1201/HMO6512, PRO; Ironside
to the War Office, 12 June 1919, WO106/1164/HMO6679,
PRO; Diary of Clarence Schey, 12 November 1918, MHC.
2. Gordon, <u>Quartered in Hell</u>, p. 247; Moore, Mead,
and Jahns, <u>Fighting the Bolsheviki</u>, p. 109.
3. Weeks Diary, 13, 17, 18 November 1918, SHSW;
Lieutenant Colonel C. Graham, 30 January 1919, "Report
on Operations, Vaga Column, November, 1918 to January,
1919," WO158/714/HMO6495, PRO; Gordon, <u>Quartered in
Hell</u>, p. 291.
4. Jones, <u>An Air-Fighter's Scrap-Book</u>, pp. 116-17;
Ironside, <u>Archangel</u>, p. 119; Livock, <u>To the Ends of
the Air</u>, p. 69.
5. Albertson, <u>Fighting Without a War</u>, p. 86;
Gordon, <u>Quartered in Hell</u>, pp. 259-82; Ullman, <u>Britain
and the Russian Civil War</u>, p. 24; Moore, Mead, and
Jahns, <u>Fighting the Bolsheviki</u>, pp. 273-81.
6. Albertson, <u>Fighting Without a War</u>, pp. 84-86;
Moore, Mead, and Jahns, <u>Fighting the Bolsheviki</u>,
p. 219.
7. Weeks Diary, 6, 7, 8 December 1918, SHSW;
Henry Katz, "Short Summary of Activities of Medical
Personnel with First Battalion 119th Infantry," no
date, MHC; Ironside to the War Office, 7 February
1919, WO158/714/HMO6495, PRO.
8. Colonel C. Graham, "Report on Operations, Vaga
Column, November, 1918 to January, 1919," 30 January
1919, WO158/714/HMO6495, PRO; Weeks Diary, 6 January
1919, SHSW; Ironside to the War Office, 7 February
1919, WO158/714/HMO6495, PRO.
9. Ironside to the War Office, 12 June 1919,
WO106/1164/HMO6679, PRO.
10. Ironside, <u>Archangel</u>, pp. 90-91.
11. Grey to Ironside, 13 June 1919,
WO106/1164/HMO6679, PRO; Shrive, <u>Diary of a P.B.O.</u>,
26 January 1919, p. 72.
12. Grey to Ironside, 13 June 1919,
WO106/1164/HMO6679, PRO; First Lieutenant E. O. Munn
to Colonel J. A. Ruggles, 16 April 1919, Records of
the American Expeditionary Forces, 1917-1923, Box 268,
RG 120, National Archives.
13. Ironside, <u>Archangel</u>, p. 89.
14. Captain Eugene Prince, "Allied Offensive

on the Vologda Force Front," 2 January 1919, M924,
reel 2.

15. H. A. Doolittle to DeWitt C. Poole, Jr.,
3 January 1919, Naval Records Collection of the Office
of Naval Records and Library, Box WA-6, RG 45; Diary
of James B. Sibley, 30 December 1918, MHC; Major M. J.
Donoghue, "Report of Engagement on December 30-31,
1918," M924, reel 2.

16. Ironside to Officer in Command, Seletskoe
Department, 12 January 1919, WO158/712, PRO.

17. H. A. Doolittle to DeWitt C. Poole, Jr.,
3 January 1919, Box WA-6, RG 45; Prince, "Allied
Offensive on the Vologda Force Front," 2 January
1919, M924, reel 2.

Chapter 7.

1. Cudahy, Archangel, p. 178; Allen F. Chew,
"Fighting the Russians in Winter: Three Case
Studies," Leavenworth Papers, no. 5 (Fort Leavenworth,
Kansas, 1981), pp. 9-10; Ironside, Archangel, p. 99.

2. Ironside to the War Office, 7 February 1919,
WO158/714/HMO6495, PRO.

3. Memorandum by Lieutenant M. Lerche,
Intelligence Officer, River Column, 13 January 1919,
WO157/1203, PRO; Colonel C. Graham, "Report of
Operations, Vaga Column, November, 1918 to January,
1919," 30 January 1919, WO158/714/HMO6495, PRO.

4. Crissman Diary, 25 December 1918, 1 January
1919, MHC; Arkins Diary 25, 26 December 1918,
1 January 1919, MHC.

5. Weeks Diary, 24, 30 December 1918, 9, 14, 15,
17, 18 January 1919, SHSW; Crissman Diary 3, 5, 6, 10
January 1919, MHC; Arkins Diary 7, 8, 9, 11, 13, 15,
17 January 1919, MHC.

6. Daniel H. Steele, "The Evacuation of
Shenkursk," The American Legion Weekly, 23 November
1923, pp. 11-12, and 23; Crissman Diary, 22 January
1919, MHC; Ironside to the War Office, 7 February
1919, WO158/714/HMO6495, PRO.

7. Colonel C. Graham, "Report on Operations, Vaga
Column, November, 1918 to January, 1919," 30 January
1919, WO158/714/HMO6495, PRO; Crissman Diary, 22, 23
January 1919, MHC; Ironside to the War Office,
22 January 1919, WO106/1153/HMO6606, PRO.

8. Colonel C. Graham, "Report on Operations, Vaga
Column, November, 1918 to January, 1919," 30 January
1919, WO158/714/HMO6495, PRO; Arkins Diary, 25
January 1919, MHC.

9. Ironside to the War Office, 25 January 1919,
WO106/1153/HMO6606, PRO; Ironside to the War Office,

7 February 1919, WO158/714/HMO6495, PRO; Ironside to
the War Office, 24 January 1919, WO106/1153/HMO6606,
PRO.
       10. Shrive, Diary of a P.B.O., 26 January 1919,
pp. 73-75; Colonel C. Graham, "Report on Operations,
Vaga Column, November, 1918 to January, 1919,"
30 January 1919, WO158/714/HMO6495, PRO.
       11. Colonel C. Graham, "Report on Operations, Vaga
Column, November, 1918 to January, 1919," 30 January
1919, WO158/714/HMO6495, PRO; Colonel C. Graham, Vaga
Column Operation Order No. 1, 24 January 1919,
WO158/714/HMO6495, PRO; Arkins Diary, 25 January
1919, MHC.
       12. Colonel C. Graham, "Report on Operations, Vaga
Column, November 1918, to January, 1919," 30 January
1919, WO158/714/HMO6495, PRO; Charles A. Thornton to
Mrs. O. M. Thornton, 23 February 1919, enclosed in
Lieutenant Colonel Edward S. Thurston to Colonel
George Stewart, 15 March 1919, Records of the American
Expeditionary Forces, 1917-1923, Box 1548, RG 120;
Memorandum by Finlayson, 16 March 1919,
WO158/714/HMO6495, PRO; Ironside to the War Office,
26 January 1919, WO106/1153/HMO6606, PRO.
       13. Chew, "Fighting the Russians in Winter,"
p. 13; Cudahy, Archangel, p. 188; Weeks Diary,
27 January 1919, SHSW; Ironside to the War Office,
12 June 1919, WO106/1164/HMO6679, PRO.

Chapter 8.

       1. Ironside to the War Office, 23 February 1919,
WO106/1153/HMO6606, PRO; Ironside, Archangel, p. 112;
J. Brooks Nichols to Stewart, 8 March 1919, penciled
notation by Stewart, Stewart Papers.
       2. Ironside, Archangel, pp. 113-14; Ironside to
Stewart, 2 March 1919, Stewart Papers.
       3. Detroit Free Press, 15 April 1919, Wisconsin
War History Commission, Clipping File, 1916-1919,
SHSW; Gerald Kloss, "When U.S. Soldiers Fought the
Russians," Milwaukee Journal, 24 November 1957.
       4. Milwaukee Journal, 2 April 1919; Milwaukee
Sentinel, 10 March 1919; Chicago Tribune, 11 April
1919, Wisconsin War History Commission, Clipping
File, 1916-1919, SHSW; Cong. Record, 66th Cong.,
1 Sess., 4461 (28 August 1919); General Order by
Colonel George Stewart, 28 January 1919, Records of
the American Expeditionary Forces, 1917-1923, Box
1554, RG 120.
       5. Ruggles to Stewart, 27 February 1919, Stewart
Papers.
       6. New York Times, 1, 5, 8, 15, 21 February 1919.

7. Stewart to the War Department, 7 January 1919, Stewart Papers; Stewart to the War Department, 17 February 1919, ibid.; Stewart to the War Department, 3 February 1919, ibid.; Stewart to the War Department, 13 February 1919, ibid.; Stewart to the War Department, 17 March 1919, ibid.

8. Moore, Mead, and Jahns, Fighting the Bolsheviki, pp. 223-30; Chicago Tribune, 11 April 1918; Captain Eugene Prince, "Report of trip to Vologda Force Front," 20 February 1919, M924, reel 2; Racine Times-Call, 17 April 1919, Wisconsin War History Commission, Clipping File, 1916-1919, SHSW.

9. Stewart to General Wilds P. Richardson, 14 June 1919, Stewart Papers.

10. Detroit Free Press, 4 July 1919, 15 April 1919, Wisconsin War History Commission, Clipping File, 1916-1919, SHSW; Washington Post, 1 July 1919, ibid.; Richardson to the Adjutant General of the Army, 23 July 1919, Records of the American Expeditionary Forces, 1917-1923, Box 268, RG 120; Poole to Acting Secretary of State Frank Polk, 31 March 1919, FRUS, 1919: Russia, p. 623.

11. Chew, "Fighting the Russians in Winter," pp. 4-9; Ironside, Archangel, pp. 121-23.

12. Lieutenant E. O. Munn to Colonel J. A. Ruggles, 1 April 1919, Records of the American Expeditionary Forces, 1917-1923, Box 1553, RG 120.

13. Chew, "Fighting the Russians in Winter," p. 8; Jackson, At War with the Bolsheviks, pp. 86-87.

14. Ironside to the War Office, 12 June 1919, WO106/1164/HMO6679, PRO.

Chapter 9.

1. Thompson, Russia, Bolshevism, and the Versailles Peace, p. 49; Long, "American Intervention," p. 61.

2. Ullman, Britain and the Russian Civil War, pp. 135-44; Thompson, Russia, Bolshevism, and the Versailles Peace, pp. 125-26; Arno J. Mayer, Politics and Diplomacy of Peacemaking, Containment and Counterrevolution at Versailles, 1918-1919 (New York, 1967), pp. 433-54; Bullitt to House, 30 January 1919, PWW 54:348-49.

3. Bliss to Wilson, 12 February 1919, enclosed in Bliss to Baker, 14 February 1919, PWW:188-92; Strakhovsky, Intervention at Archangel, p. 170; Colonel J. A. Ruggles to the War Department, 29 March 1919, Records of the American Expeditionary Forces, 1917-1923, Box 1553, RG 120.

4. Chicago _Tribune_, 11, 13 April 1919, Wisconsin War History Commission, Clipping File, 1916-1919, SHSW; Mayer, _Politics and Diplomacy_, pp. 447-49; Leonid I. Strakhovsky, _American Opinion About Russia, 1917-1920_ (Toronto, 1961), pp. 96-98; Richardson to the Adjutant General of the Army, no date, M924, reel 1.

5. Ullman, _Britain and the Russian Civil War_, pp. 172, 178-81.

6. Strakhovsky, _Intervention at Archangel_, pp. 124-27.

7. Ironside, _Archangel_, p. 123; Ironside to the War Office, 12 June 1919, WO106/1164/HMO6679, PRO; Strakhovsky, _Intervention at Archangel_, p. 196.

8. Shrive, _Diary of a P.B.O._, 16 April, 22 May 1919, pp. 83, 86.

9. Ironside, _Archangel_, pp. 126-32; Ullman, _Britain and the Russian Civil War_, p. 192; Ironside to the War Office, 12 June 1919, WO106/1164/HMO6679, PRO.

10. M. P. Dutkewish to P. I. Bukowski, 16 May 1919, M924, reel 2; Captain J. A. Harzfeld, "Report of activities of Allied Commission to exchange prisoners captured on the Northern Front and observations of conditions in Bolshevik territory," 7 May 1919, M924, reel 2.

11. Ironside to Commander of U.S. Troops, 18 April 1919, Frederick Edward Bury Papers, United States Army Military History Institute; Detroit _Free Press_, 8 July 1919, Wisconsin War History Commission, Clipping File, 1916-1919, SHSW.

12. Shrive, _Diary of a P.B.O._, 13 May, 1 June 1919, pp. 85-86.

13. Crissman Diary, 24, 31 March, 5 April 1919; Arkins Diary 30 March, 1-4 April 1919, MHC.

14. Weeks Diary, 11, 17, 22, 29 April, 2, 4, 7, 9, 18, 22, 24, 28 May 1919, SHSW; Major N. N. Scales, Complaints File, May-June 1919, Records of the American Expeditionary Forces, 1917-1923, Box 1548, RG 120.

15. Weeks Diary, 7, 8, 14, 15 June 1919, SHSW; Ironside to Stewart, 14 June 1919, Stewart Papers; Richardson to the Adjutant General of the Army, 23 July 1919, Records of the American Expeditionary Forces, 1917-1923, Box 268, RG 120.

16. Arkins Diary, 17 June 1919, MHC; Albertson, _Fighting Without a War_, p. 45; Jones, _An Air-Fighter's Scrap-Book_, pp. 113-14; Weeks Diary, 1 July 1919, SHSW.

Chapter 10.

1. Ironside, Archangel, pp. 140-41; Strakhovsky, Intervention at Archangel, pp. 188-91.

2. Ullman, Britain and the Russian Civil War, p. 179.

3. Thompson, Russia, Bolshevism, and the Versailles Peace, pp. 212-21; Ullman, Britain and the Russian Civil War, pp. 186-90.

4. The War Office to Ironside, 18 June 1919, WO106/1158/HMO6657, PRO; Ironside to the War Office, 19 June 1919, WO106/1158/HMO6657, PRO; War Office, The Evacuation of North Russia, 1919 (London, 1920), Cmd. 818, pp. 37-38.

5. "Narrative of Events in North Russia," The Evacuation of North Russia, Cmd. 818, p. 13; Jackson, At War with the Bolsheviks, pp. 154-55; Ironside, Archangel, pp. 152-53; Ullman, Britain and the Russian Civil War, pp. 190, 202 f.n.

6. Undated War Office memorandum, "Mutiny of 1st. Battalion Slavo-British Legion (Dyer's) July 7th., 1919 (Together with a short history of the origin and formation of the Battalion)," WO158/725/HMO6564, PRO.

7. Ironside to the War Office, 16 July 1919, WO106/1158/HMO6657, PRO; Jones, An Air-Fighter's Scrap-Book, pp. 138-40.

8. Strakhovsky, Intervention at Archangel, p. 207; Undated memorandum by Ironside, WO158/723, PRO; Ironside to the War Office, 18 July 1919, WO106/1158/HMO6657, PRO.

9. Ironside to the War Office, 22 July 1919, WO106/1158/HMO6657, PRO; Ironside to the War Office, 28 July 1919, WO106/1158/HMO6657, PRO.

10. The War Office to Ironside, 31 July 1919, WO158/1158/HMO6657, PRO; General Henry Wilson, Memorandum of Military Members Meeting, 29 July 1919, WO106/1158/HMO6657, PRO.

11. Ironside to the War Office, 30 July 1919, WO106/1158/HMO6657, PRO.

12. Ironside to the War Office, 1 August 1918, WO106/1158/HMO6657, PRO; Ironside to the War Office, 3 August 1918, WO106/1158/HMO6657, PRO; Ironside, Archangel, pp. 167-68.

13. Ironside, Archangel, p. 168; Jackson, At War with the Bolsheviks, p. 167; Jones, An Air-Fighter's Scrap-Book, pp. 145-46.

14. Jackson, At War with the Bolsheviks, p. 166; Ironside, Archangel, p. 180.

15. Memorandum by Major L. H. Davis, 9 September 1919, WO106/1170/HMO6705, PRO; Robert A. Kilmarx, A History of Soviet Air Power (New York, 1962), pp. 51-52; Ironside, Archangel, p. 168.

16. Altham to the Admiralty, 1 October 1919, WO158/721/HMO6538, PRO.

17. Cole to Lansing, 4 August 1919, RG 59, 124.612/80, DSNA; Lansing to Cole, 15 August 1919, ibid.

18. Cole to Lansing, 4 August 1919, RG 59, 123C673/39, DSNA; Strother to Lansing, 21 August 1919, RG 59, 125.1461/2, DSNA; Strother to Lansing, 26 September 1919, RG 59, 123C673/44, DSNA; Cole to Herbert C. Hengstler, Chief, Division of Foreign Service Administration, 10 December 1919, RG 59, 125.1461/3, DSNA; Strakhovsky, Intervention at Archangel, p. 226.

19. Altham to the Admiralty, 1 October 1919, WO158/721/HMO6538, PRO.

20. Ullman, Britain and the Russian Civil War, p. 197; The War Office to Ironside, 5 August 1919, WO106/1159/HMO6666, PRO; "Troops and Civilians Evacuated From North Russia from 1st June, 1919, to 12th October, 1919," The Evacuation of North Russia, Cmd. 818, p. 45; Altham to the Admiralty, 1 October 1919, WO158/721/HMO6538, PRO.

21. Strakhovsky, Intervention at Archangel, pp. 230-54; Footman, Civil War in Russia, pp. 206-10.

22. Cudahy, Archangel, pp. 211-13.

23. John A. Commons to Professor Carl Russell Fish, 21 May 1919, Carl Russell Fish Papers, SHSW; Eau Claire Leader, 25 July 1919, Wisconsin War History Commission, Clipping File, 1916-1919, SHSW; Richardson to the Adjutant General of the Army, 23 July 1919, Records of the American Expeditionary Forces, 1917-1923, Box 268, RG 120; Detroit Free Press, 5 July 1919, Wisconsin War History Commission, Clipping File, 1916-1919, SHSW.

24. Memorandum by Wilson, 1 December 1919, The Evacuation of North Russia, Cmd. 818, pp. 5-7.

25. Altham to the Admiralty, 1 October 1919, WO158/721/HMO6538, PRO; Halliday, Ignorant Armies, p. 218.

26. Lockhart, British Agent, p. 308.

27. Memorandum by Wilson, 1 December 1918, The Evacuation of North Russia, Cmd. 818, pp. 5-7; Cole to Francis, 1 June 1918, FRUS, 1918: Russia, 2:477.

Selected Bibliography

MANUSCRIPTS

The following collections were consulted in the preparation of this work:

Michigan Historical Collections, Bentley Historical
    Library, University of Michigan:
    Edwin Arkins Papers; Jay H. Bonnell Papers; John
    S. Crissman Papers; Henry Katz Papers; Michael
    Macalla Papers; Charles B. Ryan Papers; Clarence
    Schey Papers; James Sibley Papers; Kenneth A.
    Skellenger Papers
Missouri Historical Society:
    David R. Francis Papers
State Historical Society of Wisconsin:
    Carl Russell Fish Papers; Records of the Wisconsin
    War History Commission; Clarence J. Primm Papers;
    Glen L. Weeks Papers; William F. Whyte Papers
United States Military Academy Library, Special
    Collections Division:
    George Evans Stewart Papers
United States Army Military History Institute:
    Frederick Edward Bury Papers
    Wilds P. Richardson Papers

ARCHIVAL COLLECTIONS

National Archives of the United States:
    Record Group 45, Naval Records Collection of the
    Office of Naval Records and Library; Record Group
    59, General Records of the Department of State;
    Record Group 84, Records of the Foreign Service
    Posts of the Department of State; Record Group
    120, Records of the American Expeditionary Forces,
    1917-1923.

Public Record Office:
    War Cabinet Conclusions and Memoranda (CAB 23 and
    24); Records of the Supreme War Council (CAB 25);
    Papers of the Director of Military Operations and
    Intelligence (WO 106); Correspondence and Papers
    of Military Headquarters (WO 158); Intelligence
    Summaries (WO 157); War Diaries (WO 95).

PUBLIC DOCUMENTS

Beers, Henry P. U.S. Naval Forces in Northern Russia
    (Archangel and Murmansk), 1918-1919,
    (mimeographed). Naval Department, Office of
    Records Administration. Washington, D.C., 1943.
Department of State. Papers Relating to the Foreign
    Relations of the United States, 1918: Russia.
    3 vols., Washington, 1931-1932.
Department of State. Papers Relating to the Foreign
    Relations of the United States, 1919: Russia.
    Washington, 1937.
National Archives and Records Service. Historical
    Files of the American Expeditionary Force, North
    Russia, 1918-1919. National Archives Microfilm
    Publication M924. Washington, 1973.

BOOKS

Albertson, Ralph. Fighting Without a War: An Account
    of Military Intervention in North Russia. New
    York: Harcourt, Brace and Howe, 1920.
Black, Cyril E., ed. Rewriting Russian History:
    Soviet Interpretations of Russia's Past. New
    York: F. A. Praeger, 1956.
Bradley, John. Allied Intervention in Russia.
    London: Weidenfeld and Nicolson, 1968.
_____. Civil War in Russia, 1917-1920.
    London: B. T. Batsford, Ltd., 1975.
Cockfield, Jamie H., ed. Dollars and Diplomacy:
    Ambassador David Rowland Francis and the Fall
    of Tsarism, 1916-1917. Durham: Duke University
    Press, 1981.
Colledge, J. J. Ships of the Royal Navy: An
    Historical Index. Devon: Newton Abbot, 1969.
Cudahy, John [A Chronicler]. Archangel: The American
    War with Russia. Chicago: A. C. McClurg and
    Company, 1924.
Doolen, Richard M. Michigan's Polar Bears: The
    American Expedition to North Russia, 1918-1919.
    Ann Arbor: University of Michigan Press, 1965.

Footman, David. Civil War in Russia. London: Faber
    and Faber, 1961.
Fowler, W. B. British-American Relations, 1917-1918:
    The Role of Sir William Wiseman. Princeton:
    Princeton University Press, 1969.
Francis, David R. Russia from the American Embassy.
    New York: Charles Scribner's Sons, 1921.
Goldhurst, Richard. The Midnight War: The American
    Intervention in Russia, 1918-1920. New York:
    McGraw-Hill, 1978.
Gordon, Dennis. Quartered in Hell: The Story of the
    American North Russian Expeditionary Force,
    1918-1919. Missoula, Mont.: Doughboy Historical
    Society, 1982.
Halliday, E. M. The Ignorant Armies: The
    Anglo-American Archangel Expedition, 1918-1919.
    London: Weidenfeld and Nicolson, 1958.
Ironside, Sir William Edmund. Archangel, 1918-1919.
    London: Constable and Company, 1953.
Jackson, Robert. At War with the Bolsheviks: The
    Allied Intervention into Russia, 1917-1920.
    London: Tom Stacey, Ltd., 1972.
Jones, Ira. An Air-Fighter's Scrap-Book. London:
    Nicholson and Watson, 1938.
Kennan, George F. Russia Leaves the War. Princeton:
    Princeton University Press, 1956.
_____. The Decision to Intervene.
    Princeton: Princeton University Press, 1958.
Kilmarx, Robert A. A History of Soviet Air Power.
    New York: F. A. Praeger, 1962.
Levin, N. Gordon, Jr. Woodrow Wilson and World
    Politics: America's Response to War and
    Revolution. New York: Oxford University
    Press, 1968.
Link, Arthur S., et al., eds. The Papers of Woodrow
    Wilson. Princeton: Princeton University Press,
    55 vols., 1966-.
Livock, G. E. To the Ends of the Air. London:
    Imperial War Museum, 1973.
Lockhart, Robert Hamilton Bruce. British Agent.
    London: G. P. Putnam's Sons, 1933.
MacLaren, Roy. Canadians in Russia, 1918-1919.
    Toronto: Macmillan of Canada, 1976.
March, Peyton C. The Nation at War. Garden City,
    N. Y.: Doubleday, Doran and Company, Inc., 1932.
Mayer, Arno J. Politics and Diplomacy of
    Peacemaking: Containment and Counterrevolution
    at Versailles, 1918-1919. New York: Alfred A.
    Knopf, 1967.
Mazour, Anatole. The Writing of History in the Soviet
    Union. Palo Alto: Stanford University Press,
    1971.

Moore, Joel R., Harry H. Mead, and Lewis E. Jahns.
    The History of the American Expedition Fighting
    the Bolsheviki: Campaigning in North Russia,
    1918-1919. Detroit: The Polar Bear Publishing
    Company, 1920.
Newbolt, Henry. History of the Great War Based on
    Official Documents, Naval Operations. Vol. 5.
    London: Green and Company, 1931.
Shrive, Frank J. The Diary of a P.B.O.* Poor Bloody
    Observer. Norman Shrive, ed. Erin, Ontario:
    The Boston Mills Press, 1981.
Silverlight, John. The Victor's Dilemma: Allied
    Intervention in the Russian Civil War. London:
    Weybright and Talley, 1970.
Sivachev, N. V. and N. N. Yakovlev. Russia and the
    United States. Chicago: University of Chicago
    Press, 1979.
Soutar, Andrew. With Ironside in North Russia.
    London: Hutchinson and Company, Ltd., 1940.
Strakhovsky, Leonid I. Intervention at Archangel:
    The Story of Allied Intervention and Russian
    Counter-Revolution in North Russia, 1918-1920.
    Princeton: Princeton University Press, 1944.
    _____. American Opinion About Russia,
    1917-1920. Toronto: University of Toronto Press,
    1961.
Swettenham, John. Allied Intervention in Russia,
    1918-1919. London: George Allen and Unwin,
    Ltd., 1967.
Thompson, John M. Russia, Bolshevism, and the
    Versailles Peace. Princeton: Princeton
    University Press, 1966.
Ullman, Richard H. Intervention and the War.
    Princeton: Princeton University Press, 1961.
    _____. Britain and the Russian Civil
    War. Princeton: Princeton University Press, 1968.
Unterberger, Betty Miller. America's Siberian
    Expedition, 1918-1920: A Study of National
    Policy. Durham: Duke University Press, 1956.
    _____, ed. American Intervention
    in the Russian Civil War. Lexington, Mass.:
    D. C. Heath and Company, 1969.
Westwood, J. N. A History of Russian Railways.
    London: G. Allen and Unwin, 1964.
Williams, William Appleman. American-Russian
    Relations, 1781-1947. New York: Rinehart
    and Company, Inc., 1952.
Wise, S. F. Canadian Airmen and the First World War.
    Toronto: University of Toronto Press, 1980.

PERIODICAL LITERATURE

Altham, Edward. "The Dwina Campaign." Journal of the Royal United Service Institution 68 (February, 1923).

Bliss, Mrs. Clinton A. "Philip Jordan's Letters from Russia, 1917-1919." Missouri Historical Society Bulletin (January, 1958).

Carroll, Richard. "The Polar Bear Army." Liberty Magazine (September, 1929).

Chew, Allen F. "Fighting the Russians in Winter: Three Case Studies." Leavenworth Papers, no. 5 (Fort Leavenworth, Kansas, 1981).

Kennan, George F. "Soviet Historiography and America's Role in the Intervention." American Historical Review (January, 1960).

Kohlenberg, Gilbert C. "David Rowland Francis: American Businessman in Russia." Mid-America (October, 1958).

Long, John W. "American Intervention in Russia: The North Russian Expedition, 1918-1919." Diplomatic History (Winter, 1982).

Reed, Ernest. "The Story of the A.E.F. in North Russia." Current History (April, 1930).

Smith, Gordon W. "Waging War in 'Frozen Hell': A Record of Personal Experiences." Current History (April, 1930).

Starbuck, J. I. "The R.A.F. in Russia." The Aeroplane (July, 1919).

Steele, Daniel H. "The Evacuation of Shenkursk." The American Legion Weekly, 23 November 1923.

Trani, Eugene. "Woodrow Wilson and the Decision to Intervene in Russia: A Reconsideration." Journal of Modern History (September, 1976).

Index

About the Author

BENJAMIN D. RHODES is Professor of History at the University of Wisconsin-Whitewater. His numerous articles have appeared in such publications as *Diplomatic History, Prologue, The South Atlantic Quarterly, The Review of Politics, The International History Review,* and the *Journal of American History.*